LIQUOR, LUST,

THE STORY OF VANCOUVER'S

AND

LEGENDARY PENTHOUSE NIGHTCLUB

THE LAW

AARON CHAPMAN

Vancouver  Arsenal Pulp Press

ARSENAL PULP PRESS
Suite 101 – 211 East Georgia St.
Vancouver, BC V6A 1Z6
Canada
arsenalpulp.com

The publisher gratefully acknowledges the support of the Canada Council for the Arts and the British Columbia Arts Council for its publishing program, and the Government of Canada (through the Canada Book Fund) and the Government of British Columbia (through the Book Publishing Tax Credit Program) for its publishing activities.

Cover photograph by Brian Kent/*Vancouver Sun*
Back cover photograph (lower right) by Rebecca Blissett
Book design by Gerilee McBride
Editing by Susan Safyan
Photographs courtesy of Danny Filippone and the Penthouse Nightclub, unless otherwise indicated.

Printed and bound in Canada

Library and Archives Canada Cataloguing in Publication:

Chapman, Aaron, 1971–
    Liquor, lust, and the law: the story of Vancouver's legendary Penthouse nightclub / Aaron Chapman.

Includes bibliographical references and index.
Issued also in electronic format.
ISBN 978-1-55152-488-7

    1. Penthouse (Nightclub)—History. 2. Filippone family. 3. Nightclubs—British Columbia—Vancouver—History—20th century. 4. Bars (Drinking establishments)—British Columbia—Vancouver—History—20th century. 5. Striptease—British Columbia—Vancouver—History—20th century. 6. Vancouver (B.C.)—Social life and customs—20th century. I. Title.

TX950.59.C3C53 2012   647.95711'33
C2012-906361-4

This book is dedicated to the four brothers—Joe, Ross, Mickey, and Jimmy

Praise for

LIQUOR, LUST, AND THE LAW

"There's an old line from pantomime: 'Infamy! Infamy! They've got it all…Infamy.' Everyone from the Liquor Control Board to the Police, morally tight-assed politicians, pimps, and the occasional small-time hood had it in for the Penthouse. But it survived and continues to survive because it did something simple well: it served up sin stylishly. This book tells the dramatic and sometimes tragic story of a remarkable family, their storied venue, and a multi-generational campaign to keep the 'fun' in Vancouver." —John Belshaw, co-author of *Vancouver Noir*

"Chapman brings out all the glory and dirt of this fabled oasis of sin, covering visits in the 1950s and '60s by such giants as Duke Ellington and Nat King Cole, as well as later run-ins with the vice squad and, most notorious, the murder on the premises of the Penthouse's patriarch, Joe Phillipone, in 1983." —Brian Lynch, *Georgia Straight*

"The book pulls no punches in exploring the sometimes seamy side of city history, painting a picture of vice squads, con men and meddling politicians. Featuring period photographs and newly unearthed police documents plus many previously untold stories."
—John Lee, *InsideVancouver.ca*

"Chapman does an excellent job demonstrating the inextricable relationship between the notorious establishment and the family that poured their heart and soul into it."
—Stevie Wilson, *Scout Magazine*

"Aaron Chapman is a wonderful storyteller and he recounts the tales of celebrity high-jinks and police raids with glee. Yet what struck me most was Chapman's touching portrayal of the Filippone family. A third-generation Italian-Canadian family that has battled, worked, loved and persevered together. This is a remarkable case study on the Italian community in Vancouver and a delightful read." —Will Woods, Founder, Forbidden Vancouver Walking Tours

CONTENTS

Photo: Byron Barrett, 2012.

FOREWORD

I was about seven years old when I first walked into the Penthouse nightclub kitchen. Beyond the far doorway, I could hear music playing and people clapping and cheering. I didn't understand exactly what it was all about, but I remember thinking, This is where my dad goes to work every night! The door opened, and Dad came into the kitchen from that noisy room. All I could think of was that I wanted to go through that door. I hugged my dad, and the chef in the big white hat asked me if I wanted spaghetti, and I said yes, even though I'd eaten an hour earlier.

Dad quickly led me through the club and took me to his upstairs office. He offered me some Life Savers candy from a tray full of cigarette packages. My uncle Joe came into the office and asked me if I wanted to see him announce the next dancer on stage—of course, I said yes. This was definitely fun! We walked across the hall into a small room with a spotlight in it. He picked up a microphone and paused to look down at me and smile: "Ladies and gentlemen, it's show time in the Gold Room!" That's as far as I got that evening. Uncle Joe took me back to my dad's office.

Thirty-two years later, the memories keep coming. People often ask me about what it was like to grow up as a Filippone in Vancouver. Who did I know? Who did I meet? Did my dad personally interview the club's dancers? Even my teachers in elementary and high school would ask me to stick around after the bell to ask me about the club. Some of them—the most reserved professor types you'd least expect—would discreetly show me their special Penthouse VIP cards.

Danny Filippone enthusiastically receives the BC Entertainment Hall of Fame award on behalf of the Penthouse Nightclub.

The height of 1980s style: Penthouse drink menu with showgirl names.

It always made me laugh or smile when someone would bring up the bar.

At the age of eighteen, when most of my friends went to university, I started a busy work schedule: I had three jobs—slinging records at Kelly's Stereo Mart, punching out tickets at Exhibition Racetrack, and teaching racquetball one night a week—when I jumped on board at the Penthouse as a waiter. This meant I got to work with my uncle Joe for a couple of years before he died, which was great, and I have a lot of good memories of him. Later, when my dad asked me to work full-time at the nightclub, it was just the beginning of my adventure.

My first year of working in management was the year of Expo 86 and the place was jumping—there was lots of action and my friends were always coming by. I still had much to learn. Suddenly there seemed to be a strip bar on every corner. There were forty-two in Vancouver's Lower Mainland in the years after Expo. In the 1980s the popular trend in the exotic nightclub scene was "shower power." It must have been a good time to be a plumber installing onstage showers in strip bars! We never did that at the Penthouse, even though everyone else seemed to be.

While the Penthouse remained popular, it was beginning to look like a club still frozen in the 1960s. I tried to bring my own style and energy into the place. Throughout the 1990s and into the new millennium, I discovered ways of reinventing it, from offering Heritage Vancouver tours to hosting industry parties, opening up to movie location shoots, and participating

Once a haunt of the rich and famous,
a Seymour Street landmark perseveres
in an increasingly classless society

...e Penthouse
that Joe built

Ross Filippone
and son Danny
ensure that the
X-rated former
supper club
remains a
family affair

by Sherryl Yeager
contributing writer

On a stage where Sammy Davis Jr. once stood, a naked brunette called Athena strokes her muscled buttocks with a flaming torch.

All the women in the Penthouse nightclub are working. Sitting in seats that may have once held Gary Cooper or Ella Fitzgerald, a group of women sip mini-bottles of champagne. They talk about their last dates, scan the crowd and look available. Men of all ages and occupations file in, watch the strip show, play some pool and drink beer.

For 49 years, the Filippone family has operated

it's a stripper bar with a lot of history.

George Burns handed out cigars to the crowd on the day Danny Filippone, the current manager, was born. After Filippone's uncle and club founder Joe Philliponi (immigration officials changed his spelling) was murdered in a bungled robbery in 1983, the crowd of 800 mourners included Supreme Court justices, businessmen and dancers.

"Twenty years ago this was a classy joint because the people who went there made it a classy joint," says Filippone. "I could make this a classier joint, but look around. Who goes to a peeler bar now? It's not your big-time

Vancouver Courier cover story, January 21, 1996.

in gay and lesbian pride festivals. We found ourselves doing it all!

During this same period, the other strip bars began shutting down. Retro suddenly became a popular style, and everything old was cool again. The Penthouse, after sixty years of business, was in sync with the times, as it had been when my dad and uncles ran the business. The crowds and excitement during the 2010 Winter Olympics in Vancouver reminded us of Expo 86, and there were line-ups to get in to the club once again. In a way, the Penthouse felt re-born.

A couple of years ago my wife and I were doing some routine cleaning of the old Penthouse office when I discovered a hole in the wall—it was almost like a secret hollow compartment—that had been hidden behind an old photocopier. I telephoned my dad to ask him if he knew anything about it. He had no idea, but told me that anything I found in there we'd split fifty-fifty!

Inside, we found dozens and dozens of photographs from the club's heyday, classic snapshots taken inside the Penthouse and vintage photos of Seymour Street that Uncle Joe had hidden away for safekeeping. I recognized some of the pictures—many I'd seen in the background of other photographs of the club, and I thought they were now lost. We framed many of them and hung them back up in the bar.

At 4:15 on the morning of November 30, 2011, I got the phone call that you never want to get as a business owner. It was my manager, who lived next door to the Penthouse. When he said the word "fire," I raced down to the club with my heart pounding. I knew no one was in the building, so there was no one in jeopardy, but I wondered if this would be my last drive to the Penthouse. Would everything I'd done for the last thirty years just be gone? There was no one to talk to, and a million things were swirling around in my head.

When I arrived it looked like a scene from a movie; fire trucks, police cars, and reporters were all swarming around. The fire department eventually told me that, while there was significant damage, the building itself could be saved. So too could our huge collection of photographs—including the newly discovered ones.

We've always been proud of the history of the Penthouse, and I've wanted to do this book for many years. Both my father and uncle Joe had thought about making a book at one point, and they'd even begun to collect their notes together, but were always too busy to get very far. My mother too began to sketch out a book of her own stories about what it was like becoming part of the family, the ups and downs, and what it was like raising a new generation of Filippones. Other people as well had approached our family over the years, wanting to write a book, but they never seemed to have the right angle or want to tell the story as a whole.

I met author Aaron Chapman when he started to write an article about the Penthouse for the *Vancouver Courier* that celebrated the sixty-year anniversary since we'd been in business. Dad got to read an early version of it before he passed away. Both my dad and I agreed it was the best and most accurate article that had ever

Danny and his father Ross.

been written about the Penthouse. This, and the timely discovery of the once-lost photographs, reignited our idea about a book. I promised my dad I would see it become a reality.

The fact that the photographs—and most of all the Penthouse itself—was saved in the 2011 fire further motivated me. I wanted to see a book that told the full history of the Penthouse, one that would detail the highs and lows and the laughs and the tears over the years. I wanted a book that would not only feature our amazing collection of photographs but also tell some of the stories behind them—many of which are here in print for the very first time. The year 2013 will mark the 100th birthday of my uncle Joe. I wonder what he'd think of Vancouver if he could see it now? One thing's for sure—I know he'd be doing somersaults if he could see the Penthouse still thriving on Seymour Street, where it's always been. And I'd like to think that he and the rest of his brothers are lighting up their cigars and smiling down on the whole affair and are as pleased to see this book as I am.

On behalf of the Filippone family, I would like to give a heartfelt thank-you to all of the wonderful customers, friends, and colleagues we've met along the way. A bar is just an empty building without people in it, and none of this would have been possible without you. Thank you for all these wonderful years and memories. Enjoy!

Danny Filippone
August 2012

PROLOGUE

After the fire at the Penthouse Nightclub was put out, the joke on the street was, "While everybody knew the exotic dancers there were hot—they didn't know they'd burn the place down."

But when Vancouver's Fire and Rescue Services arrived on the scene on November 30, 2011, nobody was laughing. Thick grey-black smoke bellowed into the air, and wild orange flames roared from the back of the legendary nightclub. It was a clear, chilly night—not a drop of Vancouver's famous autumn rain to dampen the fire's rage. Crews from five nearby fire halls—forty firefighters and two battalion chiefs in total—were dispatched to the 1000 block of Seymour Street at 4:21 a.m. When Charles Mulder, a firefighter who was driving one of the trucks, rushed to the scene, the cluster of neighbourhood cars parked on the street forced him to steer sharply at Nelson Street onto Seymour and whip-shot a newspaper box on the corner, sending it flying, but soon enough he and the other firefighters were able to set up their hoses and ladders in front of the club. Battalion Chief Randy Hebenton was immediately concerned that the blaze would spread beyond the Penthouse to the very old residential house next door—one of the last of its kind downtown—or even potentially jump a short back-alleyway to other buildings on the block.

Hebenton, a thirty-five-year veteran of the department and one of its most senior tactics officers, was, luckily, one of the best men in the city to battle the blaze. Born and raised in East Vancouver and possessing a resemblance to craggy actor Richard

The Penthouse on the night of the fire, November 30, 2011. Film capture: Chris Anka, CBC Vancouver.

Three firemen in front of the Penthouse. Film capture: Chris Anka, CBC Vancouver.

Widmark, the fifty-seven-year-old firefighting veteran teaches strategies and tactics to other fire departments around the province, but it was perhaps his experience with the Penthouse itself that may have saved the building that night.

"When I was about nineteen or twenty years old, I'd go in for a beer and watch the show," he chuckles. "I hung out there a bit with some other firefighters. I hadn't been there for twenty-five years, and the building's gone through a lot of additions and renovations. But I used to date a couple of the dancers back in the day, and got invited to their dressing rooms a few times. So I was, well, let's put it this way, familiar with that part of the building."

Hebenton explains:

Because I knew the spaces in the back, I knew there was a strong potential for the fire to spread. Had the fire started in the showroom downstairs—which is a big area with a lot of oxygen—there would have been no stopping the fire; it would have quickly gotten out of control, and I doubt we could have saved the building. The boys did an excellent job of confining it to that small back room, and so we saved the structure. While there was considerable smoke damage, the building was still standing. There was certainly a feeling of accomplishment, as there always is when it goes like that.

While causes ranging from arson to faulty wiring in the 1940s-era building were considered, the subsequent investigation proved inconclusive; all that could be determined was that it started in the dancers' change room at the rear of the building. In the end, the most likely suspect was a burning cigarette that had been discarded in the trash.

The fire was first reported to emergency services by a passing Vancouver Police Department patrol car.

Fire damages Penthouse nightclub

VANCOUVER: Owner hopes to have historic strip club back in operation in two weeks

BY JOHN COLEBOURN
THE PROVINCE

Most nights at the legendary Penthouse nightclub in downtown Vancouver, the sizzle happens on the main-floor stage.

The unexpected smoke and fire this time had Vancouver firefighters battling hard early Wednesday to save the legendary strip club.

According to Vancouver Fire Department spokesman Gabe Roder, a sharp-eyed Vancouver police officer on patrol in the area noticed smoke pouring out of the roof of the maroon-coloured, two-storey building at about 4:20 a.m.

Firefighters were there within minutes and it took about an hour and a half to contain the blaze and save the landmark attraction.

Roder said fire investigators believe the blaze started in a dressing room that the strippers use in the upstairs of the building in the 1000-block Seymour Street. "The damage is significant to the upstairs change room. We are confident the fire was accidental."

Roder said the smoke and flames went through a skylight area and didn't spread downward. No one was hurt.

Danny Filippone, owner of the Penthouse, said they're hoping to be back in operation within two weeks. "We are blessed and happy they were able to save the building," he said. "Our goal is to get it open before Christmas."

The story of the Penthouse started with the Filippone family's arrival in Vancouver from the Calabria region of Italy in the late 1920s. The building was constructed in 1938, and in 1947 it became a restaurant and nightclub.

Many celebrities such as Frank Sinatra, Sammy Davis Jr., Bing Crosby, Errol Flynn and Gary Cooper frequented the club.

Eldest brother Joe Philliponi (he spelled his name differently from the rest of the family) was murdered at the nightclub in 1983.

"It is the oldest strip club in Vancouver," said Janet Leduc, executive director of the Heritage Vancouver Society. "There are so many stories about the Penthouse," she said of the club's past. "We have so few places like that left."

Randy Knowlan, owner of Stripper Entertainment, an agency that supplies dancers to the clubs, also noted that strip clubs are dying out across Metro Vancouver.

But he said strip clubs will always be around.

"A strip club is still a classic venue," he said. "Naked women are never going to go out of style."

jcolebourn@theprovince.com

Penthouse nightclub owner Danny Filippone talks Wednesday about the fire at his Vancouver strip club. The blaze began early Wednesday in an upstairs dressing room. WAYNE LEIDENFROST — PNG

And the idea that the VPD alerted fire crews to save the infamous Penthouse from burning down to an ash heap may have sent the ghosts of a few former vice-squad inspectors, who'd spent their whole careers investigating the nightclub, spinning in their graves.

For days afterward, the Penthouse fire was one of the top stories on local radio and television newscasts, and every report referred to the nightclub as "legendary" and "historic." For people who'd never been to the Penthouse, the media's use of these words made it clear that, from its after-hours speakeasy days to its place as one of Vancouver's top show lounges, the club was visited by many celebrities, including big-name

Vancouver Province,
December 1, 2011.

Opinions had always been divided about the controversial club.

Hollywood actors and actresses. Legendary musicians and performers, including Louis Armstrong and Frank Sinatra, entertained crowds from the club's stage or at private parties held in mysterious upper floors and back rooms. Colourful stories told of police raids for illegal alcohol, a notorious murder investigation, and the club's association with one of the most sensational trials the city had ever seen. Every report mentioned the Filippone family, who had operated the nightclub for more than sixty years and through two generations.

Online responses to the news stories varied from the humorous—"I bet the firefighters didn't take long to get there!"—to those who hoped the business would soon be back on its feet—"The Penthouse deserves a historic [recognition] in Vancouver"—to the contrarily unimpressed—"We actually call a strip club historic!?" Others were more blunt: "[They] should have let it burn…clean up the area."[1] Opinions had always been divided about the controversial club.

The Penthouse legend does not begin with the flashing emergency lights of Vancouver fire engines flooding onto Seymour street, or the flashing lights of those of the VPD patrol cars that repeatedly screeched up to the building since 1947, but with the story of an Italian family's immigration to Canada in the 1920s.

The Filippone family traces its roots from San Nicola da Crissa in the Calabria area in southern Italy. The toe in the "boot" of the country, today Calabria is one of the most popular regions for tourism in the country and has a large export market for its incomparable olives and olive oil, meats and cheeses. But in the early part of the twentieth century, Calabria was a poor province that shackled its citizens with near-feudal laws, making it difficult for farmers to own land. Leaving their homeland and starting elsewhere seemed to be the only choice for many southern Italians, and in the 1890s a wave of emigration from Italy began.

By 1915, five million Italians had left their country.[2] The majority of these emigrants were from *Il Mezzogiorno*, the name for the southern provinces of the country such as Calabria. They settled in other parts of Europe and as far away as Australia, Argentina, Brazil, the United States, and Canada. Giuseppe and Maria Rosa Filippone were probably typical of the thousands of new citizens who arrived in Canada in 1921. Giuseppe, a coal miner in Italy, joined hundreds of other new immigrants attracted to Vancouver Island by the promise of work in coal baron Robert Dunsmuir's mines. Filled with workers from around the world, the mines echoed with the accents of Italians, Finns, Scots, Welsh, and "Geordies" from the Tyneside region of Newcastle. All would have been heard talking and shouting orders at the colliery.

Giuseppe arrived first and settled into the small mining town of Extension, near Nanaimo, British Columbia. Maria Rosa followed a few months later

I.
BELLA FORTUNA

Maria Rosa and Giuseppe Filippone in the late 1920s.

Joe Philipponi, late 1930s.

Ross, Giuseppe, and Mickey Filippone, 1930s.

with their young son Joseph (who had come into the world, appropriately enough, after a New Year's Eve party on January 1, 1913). In Extension, Joe began to contribute to the family's income as a garment worker, making six dollars a week. He was the first member of his family to learn English, and it became his job to greet neighbours to the home, receive deliveries for the family, or talk to passersby; this may have taught Joe the "welcoming skills" that were of such great use to him later in life as the host of a club.

Joe was different than the rest of his family also because of the spelling of his name. At one point, it was wrongly alleged that Philliponi spelled his name differently as an alias or to confuse law enforcement agents. But, in fact, an immigration officer had misspelled it as "Philliponi" when he first entered Canada. The mistake was never legally corrected, and the name stuck. Eventually, Joe would come to stand out in other ways.

Coal mining was hard and dangerous work, and many miners died underground. The Extension miners came to know that the long blast on the mine's whistle could only mean bad news. The disaster at the nearby Esplanade coal mine that had taken 150 lives more than thirty years earlier in 1887 would not have been forgotten by the community. To this day known as the worst mining disaster in the history of British Columbia, the accident and its victims were remembered on each anniversary in May with a reunion of miners from around the island and a two-minute moment of silence.

The warmth of the Calabrian sun must have seemed far away on rainy Vancouver Island, but the Filippones settled into Extension, and their family quickly grew. A second boy, Jimmy Filippone, was born in 1922, followed by a third son, Ross—a name popular with the Scottish miners of Extension (and also a respectful nod to Maria *Rosa*)—just over a year later. Domenic "Mickey" Filippone was born in 1924, and Giuseppe and Maria Rosa were graced with their final child ("at last a daughter!") whom they named Florence, born in 1929.

The Filippone family not long after they arrived in Vancouver, mid-1930s. L to R: Florence, Giuseppe, Jimmy, Joe, Ross, Maria Rosa, and Domenic (Mickey).

Joe Philliponi and one of the Diamond Cabs fleet in front of Eagle Time's offices, 1942.

The mine's fortunes declined after the stock market crash, and the Filippones decided to move to the burgeoning city of Vancouver, hoping that the Lower Mainland offered a brighter future than the coal mines of Extension. In May of 1932, Giuseppe and Maria Rosa purchased their house, which still stands at 1033 Seymour Street.[3] While the younger brothers attended King George High School, Ross and Joe were called upon to supplement the family income during the Depression. Ross worked down the block at Chapman's Bowling Alley on Helmcken Street as a pinsetter, and Joe had a paper route and delivered packages as a bicycle courier. After literally saving his pennies, Joe bought a motorcycle and was soon one of the fastest couriers in town. His father and Jimmy drove delivery trucks, and so the family's first company, Eagle Time Delivery Systems Ltd., was begun in 1935.

"Joe had the city divided up into zones on a map," Ross recalled. "[It wasn't] much different [from] how transit works today. You bought these zone tickets depending on how far away you needed things delivered. It was a good system."

The Filippone home on Seymour Street was not only the base for family gatherings, but also for its business and administrative operations for the next forty years. Their backyard was a taxi and truck depot, and they ran a dispatch office from the front of the house. As business began to flourish, Eagle Time branched out with a fleet of taxicabs they called Diamond Cabs. "We Circle the City" was the company's motto. The trucking and taxi companies bolstered the family's revenue, and the Filippones soon bought the empty lot next door to their house for $1,400. Construction on the building that would become the Penthouse started in 1941. "I remember the contractors putting up the bricks," said Ross. "When the building was finished in 1942, we moved the taxi and trucking business out of the family house and into there."

Joe Philliponi's press debut (in what would be a lifetime of making headlines) appeared in the February 14, 1942 edition of the *Vancouver Sun*. A smiling Joe is

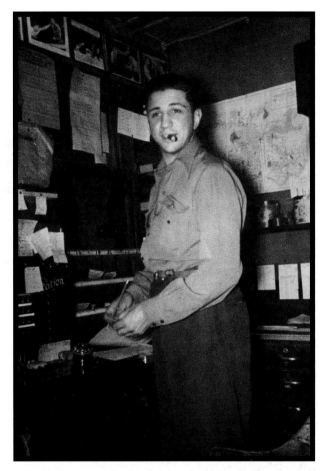

Jimmy Filippone in the Eagle Time dispatch office.

Eagle Time and Diamond Cabs building on Seymour Street, 1942.

shown as the "Happy & Proud" owner of Eagle Time below the headline, "Fast Growing Delivery Service and Cab Business in Modern Building."[4] Philliponi had built the Penthouse in contra deals with local construction supply companies in exchange for free cartage from Eagle Time Delivery. One wonders if Joe gave the reporter some complimentary cab rides in return for sterling press, because at times the tone of the article reads like an advertisement: "As soon as a customer or visitor enters the new building he senses the type of service that is maintained. A luxuriously furnished waiting room is there if one is to wait for a cab or other service, but the facilities…are all as business like and modern as they can be." Jimmy Filippone was photographed seated at the busy switchboard, as acting dispatcher. "The facilities 'behind the scenes' are no less modern than in the front offices. With a large staff of girl messengers as well as boys, the most complete arrangements have been made for their comfort…the girls have a nice powder room and lounge, with private lockers in which each can keep her own personal belongings."

At the bottom of the same page there are a number of accompanying ads from companies that Eagle Time did business with or that Philliponi bartered with in the construction of the new building, all offering their best wishes for the business at its new location, suggesting how many friends and business contacts the family had garnered in Vancouver just a little over a decade after moving there.

The Eagle Time offices may have seemed rather ostentatious for a taxi dispatch and delivery service; it was almost as if Joe already had bigger plans. The *Sun* article concluded prophetically that the spacious new building "should take care of the development of the business for some time to come."

It wasn't a nightclub yet, but the Filippones were already making sure that their block on Seymour Street was a hub of activity. The family's interest in sports

Jimmy, right, gives an Eagle Time athletic jacket to a young athlete. Photo: Vancouver Public Library Archives, 81118.

Joe at Christmas Party at Eagle Time, 1949. Photo: Vancouver Public Library Archives, 81118G.

I. Bella Fortuna

Joe and the Eagle Time Athletic Club boys, Christmas 1949. Photo: Vancouver Public Library Archives, 81118B.

first brought social activities into the building.

"We had a lot of room in there," Ross recalled. "So that's when we decided to put a gymnasium in and started a boxing club for the neighbourhood kids. It was one of the best-known clubs in the city. We had more champions than you could shake a fist at. We sponsored lacrosse and basketball, football, bowling, and we hosted a Christmas carnival for the kids, too. It was almost like a community centre."

Eagle Time already had its in-house stars: Jimmy

Jimmy Filippone, Charlie
Bagnato, and Pops Yates at
Eagle Time, c. 1941.

was a two-time finalist in the BC Golden Gloves boxing
championship. Between 1938 and 1942, he was one
of the leading amateur lightweights and had bouts
against well-known boxers such as Jimmy Crook,
Henry Devine, and Robert Hickey. A generation of
Vancouver youth in the late 1930s and '40s passed
through Eagle Time Athletics and learned to box from
Jimmy and coaches like Val Roach and Pops Yates.

Ross and Mickey had potential to become
professional bowlers and helped coach young people

Ross in uniform, 1940.

While Ross and Joe were in the Air Force, Maria, Giuseppe, Jimmy, Florence, and Mickey ran the business.

and others interested in the sport. Meanwhile, Joe—never much of a sportsman unless it involved betting on a horse—was "Uncle Joe" to the hundreds of children who came to the gym at Eagle Time, including former Vancouver City Councillor George Puil, who would go on to be a University of British Columbia Sports Hall of Fame inductee in football and rugby, "Whistling" Bernie Smith, who Joe would encourage to become a policeman,[5] and "Socking" Sid Morrisroe, who first competed at a Silver Gloves boxing tournament at the Eagle Time gym and would years later appear again in the history of the Penthouse in a notorious role less befitting a champion.

The outbreak of World War II directly touched Vancouver's Italian community when more than 1,800 living in the city were designated as "enemy aliens" after the fascist Prime Minister Benito Mussolini joined forces with Nazi Germany.[6] The Italian consulate in Vancouver encouraged local Italians to declare their allegiance to Mussolini, and forty-four men in the community were removed to Ontario internment camps. Because Joe had been born in Italy, it's likely he would have come under initial scrutiny from government authorities during the implementation of the War Measures Act. But Joe—and many others in the community—made their loyalties to Canada clear with the help of Angelo Branca.

A legend in Vancouver legal history—the city's first Italian lawyer and judge—Branca formed the Italian-Canadian War Vigilance Association. He sent 2,000 flyers around East Vancouver to announce a mass

Joe in the RCAF, c. 1943.

meeting for June 10, 1940 at the Hastings Auditorium. That morning, North Americans heard the news that Mussolini had declared war on the allies, and by nightfall about 400 people—Joe Philliponi among them—attended Branca's rally where they cheered a resolution that publicly announced that all members of the association were unequivocally behind Canada's war efforts. Joe Philliponi and Angelo Branca became friends, and the legal counsel Branca provided to the

Jimmy, Giuseppe, Ross (in uniform), Maria Rosa, and Mickey.

Filippones over many years would prove invaluable.

In 1942, inspired by feelings of Canadian patriotism, both Joe and Ross signed up for the Royal Canadian Air Force. Jimmy was left in charge of keeping the family business running and helped to keep an eye on Mickey, who had begun skipping classes at school in order to go to the horse races. Joe was posted at Jericho Beach Air Station, where his experience with the taxi company seemed to make him a natural for assignment to the motor pool. Ross worked in the transport division of the RCAF, driving trucks.

Joe was never sent overseas, but friends would say that he didn't go through the war without seeing any action. One night in 1944, Joe stood in the lineup for a movie at the Vogue Theatre in Vancouver, his sergeant's stripes on one arm and his date on the other. The patron in front of him seemed to be taking an unreasonably long time to purchase his tickets, so Joe asked him to hurry it up. The man angrily turned around with a gun in his hand—he was in the process of robbing the box-office cashier. Local newspaper columnist Denny Boyd later joked that "whether [it was] from bravado, fear, or indignation at seeing someone's gate receipts being pilfered,"[7] Joe then wrapped his arms around the hold-up man, wrestled him to the ground, and held him until the police arrived.

After the war, Joe and Ross returned to work at Eagle Time. In 1949, their father, who had been suffering from emphysema for years from working and breathing the black dust in the coal mines of Nanaimo,

Joe and Ross, 1946, at
the Penthouse.

passed away. The loss of her husband was hard on
Maria Rosa and her children. Now Joe, the eldest son,
took on the role of head of the family. Both he and Ross
had bigger ideas than just running a taxi company with
a gym on the side.

"When the war was over, I thought about studying
law, but I was also interested in the restaurant
business," said Ross. "Joe had some ideas too…"

The Penthouse originated in a Vancouver much different than today's. Those who frequent the Granville Entertainment District, one of Gastown's wine bistros, or a Commercial Drive watering hole, would scarcely recognize Vancouver in the post-war years.

Downtown Vancouver was not the metropolis of glass towers it is now. Only the Sun Tower, Marine Building, and the old Hotel Vancouver edged the skyline to compete with the backdrop of the North Shore Mountains across the Burrard Inlet. Instead, smoke coughed from smokestacks and churned from the mills and rail yards in False Creek. Most downtown city blocks looked more like the residential Strathcona neighbourhood does today, with smaller two-storey houses occupied by families with multiple children.

Before every house had a television set, these families sat on their verandas in the evenings, reading newspapers, watching children play, or gossiping with the neighbours over fences, as music or shows from a Philco radio were heard through an open window. Fathers played catch with sons in small front yards and, in the mornings, headed to work, nearly all of them wearing hats. It wasn't just that the city was smaller—the population of greater Vancouver was 562,462 in 1951, compared to more than 2.3 million in 2012[8]—but places where a fellow might socialize for a drink when the sun went down and enjoy an evening of cocktails and good cheer were not easy to find. When Welsh poet Dylan Thomas visited Vancouver in April 1950, he called the city a "handsome hellhole"

II. WHAT DOES A GUY HAVE TO DO TO GET A DRINK AROUND HERE?

View from the Penthouse, c. 1970s, over downtown Vancouver.

The beer parlours reeked of… smoke and stale beer.

and complained about the "pious and patriotic" people of British Columbia who he thought acted more British than the Brits back home.[9] Thomas decried the local bars that legally couldn't serve whiskey or wine, closed on holidays, and were open for what seemed like just a few hours each day.

For much of its history—though it was the same frontier town that began in 1867 when Gassy Jack Deighton offered the local mill workers all they could drink in return for helping him to construct the bar that the city would be built around—Vancouver has been divided, over the decades, about liquor.

British Columbia experimented briefly with prohibition from 1917 to 1921. After World War I, the provincial government regulated the sale of alcohol at government liquor stores. By the 1920s, public support for establishments that sold beer by the glass was broad enough that the government eased restrictions and the province's three-member Liquor Control Board created the beer parlour in March 1925.

These establishments purposely offered little to encourage a patron to have a pleasant night out. Even the term "parlour" was a misnomer, for it promised some measure of comfort that was never fulfilled—they were dreary places. As author Daniel Francis notes, the beer parlours reeked "of stale tobacco, smoke and stale beer … There was no standing at the bar, no hard liquor, no entertainment [i.e., no music either from a radio or musicians], no singing or darts or billiards, nothing to suggest that the consumption of alcohol might be enjoyable."[10]

For a brief period, women were not allowed in beer parlours. Then in 1927, separate rooms were granted to accommodate women drinking alone or with escorts. Hotel beer parlours were also required to place a partition between the men's and ladies' sections as well as separate entrances; with a rise in reports of venereal disease during the 1930s, worried puritanical authorities suspected that the beer parlours were black holes of venereal disease-ridden prostitutes.

Given the restrictions on Vancouver's nightlife at the time, it might be easy to assume that there was no taste for alcohol in British Columbia except for a ruffian minority—which certainly wasn't the case. It was still legal to drink at private residences, so bootleggers and clubs that were not considered open to the public thrived. There, members signed in upon entry, and these "private" establishments managed to skirt the liquor laws of the time.

The Eagle Time Athletic Club would be the beneficiary of the city's thirsty citizens. Joe built another floor at the top of the Eagle Time building and used it as a lavish apartment for himself. With business doing well and post-war prosperity in the air, Joe's characteristic generosity and gregariousness found a greater outlet. He began to host after-hours parties in the upstairs apartment and, for a donation of $1.75 (to the purchase of sports equipment for the gym), one was granted entry.[11]

There were no bar liquor licences in British Columbia at the time. Even at the elegant Hotel Vancouver's Panorama Roof, guests brought their own liquor in

The original Penthouse bar.

Ross at the Palomar Supper Club, one of Vancouver's now-lost ballrooms. The Filippones got their show-business start booking the Palomar with Sandy DeSantis.

brown bags. The difference was, at Joe's apartment and certainly later at the Penthouse, if you were in a pinch and showed up with nothing, something could be conveniently supplied from a back room. Soon the Seymour Street building wasn't attracting just the local kids who wanted to learn how to box, but their mothers and fathers, who now stopped in at night after the gym had closed.

The Palomar Ballroom at 713 Burrard Street, which opened in 1937, was just another popular bottle club,[12] and the sort of place in which people would have danced all evening, before ending the night at Joe's apartment. The King Cole Trio, the Ink Spots, Frankie Laine, the Mills Brothers, Louis Armstrong, Duke Ellington, Jerry Colonna, and Nellie Lutcher all performed there in the 1940s, as did orchestra leader Sandy DeSantis, who had taken the Palomar over from owner Hymie Singer. "Sandy made a bundle of money off of those servicemen coming through during the war. But after the war was over, the servicemen disappeared," said Ross Filippone. "He loved to gamble and drink, but the money wasn't coming in anymore, and he was having difficulties financially when he came to us." Eager to get involved in the club business, Joe and Ross made a deal with DeSantis and became equal partners with him in the Palomar. But DeSantis's gambling habit put him deeper and deeper in debt.

"We eventually bought his house to get him out of the hole he'd dug himself in," Ross recalled. What Joe and Ross learned from the Palomar experience was

Bill Kenny & the Ink Spots with Sandy DeSantis at the Palomar Supper Club, c. 1940s.

Joe (L.) and Sandy DeSantis smooch with Carmen Miranda.

not so much to be careful of one's business partners (DeSantis remained a family friend and Penthouse regular for years afterward), but a lesson in the value of real estate. "We'd just spent $100,000 renovating and decorating the place in a Grecian style, with columns of red and gold, when the owners of the Palomar came in and told us to get out in thirty days because they'd sold the building and were going to put up an office block. After that experience, we learned there was no way we were going to get into a property we didn't own. You have to own your own place."

Thanks to developers, the Palomar would never become the busy nightspot the Filippones hoped it would be. And, thanks to the Vancouver police, Joe's after-hours apartment nightspot almost didn't get started. On July 26, 1947, a twenty-man police squad of uniformed officers and fedora and trench-coat-clad detectives pushed their way through the front door of the Eagle Time building. When they shouted "Vancouver police!", the music on the record player stopped. Flashbulbs exploded light on to the blinded and squinting men and women seated at tables, trying to hide their gins and whiskies. The police confiscated bottles of booze hidden by those in attendance or stashed behind Philliponi's apartment bar—forty-nine bottles of liquor and 467 bottles of beer. "The largest liquor seizure in a decade," reported the *Vancouver Sun*. The Penthouse had been the target of its first police "dry squad" raid and Joe was charged with violating the Government Liquor Act.

The squad asserted that the penthouse apartment,

which was Joe's home, was being operated as a public place and that the $1.75 donation was, in fact, an admission fee. Joe maintained that the fee went primarily to the boys athletic club, and helped cover the cost of soft drinks at the late night parties he was increasingly famous for hosting.

In a *Vancouver Sun* article from that same year, columnist Hal Straight painted a vivid picture of what it was like to visit Joe's penthouse apartment. You can almost hear the laughter, glasses clinking, and Artie Shaw's "Begin the Beguine" on Joe's record player.

"Positively no liquor on the premises" at the Penthouse: Mickey (centre) with two friends.

Visiting the plush penthouse is like wading through a slimy marsh and coming out on a beautiful emerald lake. You go from drab, dirty Seymour Street into a building and pass by a dispatching office which guides the Diamond Cabs and Eagle Time Transfer vehicles, up a flight of narrow stairs up to the third floor—just recently built—that stretches the whole length of the premises from the front to the lane. You go into a short entrance hall and into a bar that would compete with any of its size from here to New York, with its top red velvet under glass, the walls and ceilings mirrored. The stools are tall, with round leather seats, ship deck floors, and laid veneer and expensive drapes. It has a player piano in one corner and a record player set at the side of a modern fireplace. Off the bar is a spacious lounge, well appointed with expensive chesterfield sets and coffee tables. The lights are soft, and the rugs softer. After that there is a complete apartment suite, featuring twin beds, the colours of which are a long way from Seymour Street. The suite has the latest, most expensive luxury. This is Joe Philliponi's home, he says.

Lively Joe, a bachelor like his brothers, likes the name of BC's number No. 1 Playboy, as evidenced by the number of autographed pictures of entertainers under the bar's glass top. The usual inscription over lovely legs is "to my pal Joe." Each evening, he holds forth in his castle instead of the Palomar or other nightclubs where he used to do his entertaining and "Hip Hips" as his guests drop in. According to Joe, each person has to write his name on their own bottle and put it behind the bar. He provides what he calls a promotion manager to serve out these bottles and supply mixers.

Apparently, of late it has become a very popular after nightclub spot, especially with some leading business men and some high government officials. "I just love people," says Joe. "I love to have them around me and someday, if we have cocktail bars, I'll have a head start."[13]

Joe, 1947, sporting some of his famous fashion sense.

Whether some of Philiponi's well-to-do patrons discreetly did some backroom persuasion, or it was the result of the defense lawyer's successful pleading, Police Magistrate Mackenzie Matheson threw the charges out of court. The incident did not deter either Joe or the rest of the Filippones. In fact, later that year, they enterprisingly took the free publicity from the raid and successful court decision and renamed their after-hours club "The Penthouse."

Police kept up the pressure and in 1948, Joe was found guilty of consuming liquor in a public place and fined $100. Mickey Filippone, then twenty-four years old, was convicted of keeping liquor for sale (a.k.a. bootlegging) and fined $500. Joe was given another fine of $300 for a liquor violation in 1949.

However, on August 10, 1950, Vancouver City Council narrowly approved the Penthouse's application for a business licence, despite the opposition of Police Chief Walter Mulligan who was run out of town five years later in a sensational scandal over police corruption. While the Penthouse could now advertise itself as a cabaret and nightclub, it still couldn't sell liquor. After three months' renovation, the club re-opened, but enjoyed only one night's unfettered operation as a legal business to the public before the Vancouver Police paid another visit on December 3, 1950. Just two nights earlier, a special preview of

the recently renovated premises, featuring a roving searchlight at the front door and a VIP dinner, was held for local reporters, well-wishers, and friends of the Filippone brothers. Doors opened to the public the next night at nine, with musician James Drew performing on the Hammond organ. The nightclub was already taking dinner reservations for "fine Italian foods and fried chicken" (the latter supplied from the Dixie Inn Chicken Shack next door). It billed itself as "Canada's

Joe and Ross host a typical busy night at the Penthouse with members of the Mills Brothers band, restaurateur Big Frank Ross (back row, right), and *Vancouver Sun* columnist Jack Wasserman, third man to the left of Ross, in glasses. Note beer bottles and Vat 69 whiskey on table.

The Dixie Inn Chicken Shack supplied food for guests of the Penthouse club in the 1940s until the early 1960s.

Most Intimate Night Club" and stayed open until a surprisingly late five a.m.

Following a successful Saturday night's business at around 3:45 Sunday morning, when the club was still packed with patrons, the police dry-squad again raided the club. This time, their haul would be just two bottles of liquor. Either the patrons had finished off most of what they'd brown-bagged or nobody bothered to look underneath the tablecloths to see the little ledges on the table legs that were just the perfect height and width to hold a bottle. Of course, when asked, Philliponi would innocently maintain that these were made to hold ladies' purses.

The Penthouse in the 1950s began to distinguish itself from the rest of Vancouver's nightlife. Its reputation as a place where you could get a drink at a late hour helped—even the liquor raids acted as free promotion. But it became known as the spot where, after other nightclubs had closed, club owners, waitresses, barmen, dancers, musicians, probably a few off-duty police officers, and night-shift newspaper reporters ended the night. And it was known not just to the locals, but to a growing array of touring musicians and actors making appearances in Vancouver for film premieres or performing in shows.

"Before the days of limousines, we used Diamond Cabs for our artists," recalled pioneering concert promoter Hugh Pickett. "We always brought them to the Penthouse. In those days, it was the only place to get a decent meal—and a drink—after a concert. Practically anybody who came to Vancouver went there."[14] Pickett escorted celebrities including Victor Borge, Ella Fitzgerald, Harry Belafonte, Robert Goulet, Ricardo Montalban, Myrna Loy, Pat Boone, and Jimmy Durante to the Penthouse.

Frank Sinatra himself announced from the stage at the end of his 1957 Orpheum show in Vancouver, "That's it, everybody. See you all at the Penthouse!" The audience rushed out to the club, two blocks away, where a line-up quickly formed on Seymour Street. When Sinatra arrived, Ross and Mickey Filippone had to sneak him in the back door. "I just wish he'd done it on a slow night," laughed Ross. "We were already busy that evening!"

III. ON WITH THE SHOW

Ella Fitzgerald (centre, front) at the Penthouse, with Sandy DeSantis (third from left) and Joe (far right).

Joe, Harry Belafonte, Mickey, and Ross, 1961. Belafonte "officiated" at a mock wedding ceremony for Ross and Penny at the club after this photo was taken.

"Everybody knew you went to the Penthouse after a show, so it seems like nobody got there before midnight or one a.m. If you were in the music business, you knew there was going to be a jam session [after a concert] at the Penthouse," recalls eighty-four-year-old Edna Randle. Her memories bring a smile and youthful sparkle to her face as she recalls the many nights that seemed to end on Seymour Street. Born and raised in Vancouver, Edna was in her twenties when

Billie Holiday (left) with
Joe and his girlfriend (later
fiancée) Shirley Meikle.

she began working as a record company publicist and
wholesale representative for Columbia, Capitol, and
RCA Records. "I knew everybody at the radio stations
and newspapers. Musicians who were in town either
recording or performing, I would…show around on
behalf of the record label. So I was at the Penthouse just
about every weekend," Randle says.

The Penthouse also became a favourite nightspot
for local musicians to unwind with a drink after

Ross with bandleader Les Brown in the 1950s.

L to R: Joe, his girlfriend Shirley, jazz singer Herb Jeffries, and Sandy DeSantis.

their gigs. "The musicians were often just playing big band standards at their paying gigs at the Hotel Vancouver's Panorama Roof or dances at the Commodore Ballroom," recalls Edna. "But I'd often see them perform the music they personally wanted to play at the Penthouse, after-hours. There was always something happening there."

One of Randle's favourite memories is of the night in 1950 when the legendary Canadian pianist Oscar Peterson squared off at the piano with local pianist Chris Gage. A central figure in the early Vancouver jazz scene, Gage was considered to be one of the best musicians in Canada in the 1950s and '60s. He performed frequently at the Cave nightclub, where his playing was often hailed as "genius," but because he seldom toured, died young—only thirty-seven—from an overdose, and left very little recorded material, he never became a household name in international jazz circles.

"Chris and his regular bassist Stan 'Cuddles' Johnson were in there darn near every night," Edna says. "Every tour that came through tried to get Chris to join the band, and he never wanted to leave Vancouver. He was really the equivalent of Oscar Peterson in skill, so to see the two of them together at the upstairs piano at the Penthouse, with Oscar playing for a bit, then Chris playing for a bit—trading off, back and forth—the two of them laughing as they were playing was something I'll never forget. Oscar said later that Chris Gage was the only pianist he feared."

Edna also remembers the night trumpeter and

bandleader Harry James came (without his wife, the actress Betty Grable) to the Penthouse. "James sat upstairs at a big table," she remembers. "People kept coming over to the table and joining in—he didn't know half of them, but was being social. At the end of the evening, he was presented with the bill. Oh! What a change in demeanour! All those people had left their drinks and meals on his tab. He didn't say anything, but paid up and walked out. I thought, that wasn't nice—I knew some of the people who went to that table and didn't chip in and who easily could have."

Edna adds, "Joe Philliponi was a real friend to the musicians. I remember one very well-known Vancouver musician in the '50s had been involved in a car accident that had caused a fatality. Behind the scenes, Joe helped get him a lawyer."

She also remembers the night Louis Armstrong came to the Penthouse with his band, including singer Velma Middleton and trombonist Jack Teagarden. "Louis didn't play, he just went to the back with Joe. I thought Joe had a gentlemen's club up there but figured it had nothing to do with gentlemen! But Jack hung around out front, talking with people and, God bless him, he wanted me to sit beside him." In the same room upstairs where Peterson and Gage had played a couple of years earlier, Teagarden entertained his listeners with a song called "A Hundred Years from Today." One might even imagine Teagarden adding a wink to his sleepy vocal delivery when he came to the line in the song that went, "Why crave a penthouse that's fit for a Queen?"

The Cave floorshow girls, c. 1950s, including Penny Marks, upper right.

Joe with the Deep River Boys, 1948.

Louis Armstrong, Ross, and jazz vocalist Velma Middleton.

"Jack was a large guy," Edna says, "and—I'll always remember this—he sang the song sitting down, holding his trombone. He undid his belt and unzipped his pants because he wanted to breathe. I guess it was easier to sing with his pants undone. I thought if the cops walked in right then they would have wondered what the heck was going on!"

While Randle was left to imagine Armstrong misbehaving upstairs that night, Ross recalled what actually happened. "Louis really loved Italian food. He came in hungry and went to our kitchen, put on an apron, even a chef's hat, and started making his own spaghetti sauce, pushing our cook out of the way. It was really comical. The chef was standing there with nothing to do while Louis was busy stirring the sauce. What are you going to do, push Satchmo out of the way?"

The Filippones' relationship with Armstrong went back to their Palomar days, when they'd also assisted with bookings on other Canadian dates. "We took Satchmo on a one-week tour," said Ross. "We first had dates with him here in Vancouver and then one week on the road in the Northwest. We flew with Louis and his whole band to Trail, BC, where he played an arena there. There wasn't even a proper runway, but it was a big deal, with the Mayor present. The only place we had a problem was Seattle, because blacks couldn't stay in hotels there. But we had an advance man a few days ahead of us to smooth things out."

The Filippones' Penthouse was one of the few venues in Vancouver to not only welcome African-American entertainers but to house and entertain them as well. Armstrong had once infamously not been permitted to stay at the Hotel Vancouver; it was then their policy not to allow "negroes."[15]

In the mid-1950s, Ross and Mickey brought the legendary black vocal group the Mills Brothers to Vancouver's Commodore Lanes to bowl. "We were bowling for two bottles of Seagram's for the winner," recalled Ross.

Joe with the Mills Brothers group and friends.

Macy's Bowling Champions, 1950: Mickey Duina, Mickey Filippone, Jimmy Filippone, Frank Iaci (a cousin of the Filippones), and Joe Duina.

Afterward, we took the boys over to celebrate at the Quadra Club. When we came in to get seated, the owner, Gordon Towne, asked me, "Do you mind if I put you guys in the VIP room?" I didn't think anything of it. I thought he figured we wanted some privacy.

We sat there and had dinner and relaxed. But I felt kind of suspicious; there weren't really a lot of people there that night.

He came over later and said, "Ross, I'm gonna tell you the truth—my patrons in the club would be highly offended if they saw a black person sitting in the main room."

"Well," I said, "Gordon, we're not going to do any business anymore—this is embarrassing"—and we left.

Ross and Don Mills from the Mills Brothers. "We were bowling for two bottles of Seagram's for the winner."

As with Armstrong, Sammy Davis Jr's relationship with the Filippone brothers went back to the days at the Palomar club when he made $500 a week with the

Sammy Davis Jr (fourth from right) and friends, including Joe and Ross (back row, right), and Mickey (seated, front).

Will Mastin Trio. Davis hit it off with Joe and the rest of the brothers, and the trio stayed in spare rooms at the family house next door during their engagements, and Maria Rosa Filippone made enough food for them all.

"Sammy Davis Jr never really smoked or drank much until he hooked up with the Rat Pack," recalled Ross. "But [even then] he never drank as much as people thought—same with Sinatra. Those guys couldn't do that and still perform. Mind you, they did a lot of other things that we wouldn't do—like smoking pot. All the musicians did."

The photo of Davis's trio and the Filippones captures not only the quality of their friendship but how colour

Boxer Max Baer, Joe, and actor Gary Cooper, 1952.

Joe with World Heavyweight Champion Joe Louis.

blind the owners and regulars of the Penthouse were compared to much of the rest of society at the time. In the photo Joe, Ross, and Mickey hold court while Davis Jr is seated with white women sitting around him and one on his lap. An Asian woman to Joe's right holds hands with a white man. Even if the revelry is fuelled by a few bottles from Joe's stash, this is one of far too few photos in this period of Vancouver's history that show the colour-line being broken with such good humour—on what appears to be a typical night at the Penthouse.

Gary Cooper (star of the 1951 film *High Noon*) visited Vancouver a half dozen times over the years for film premieres, publicity tours, or just to visit friends such as Orpheum Theatre impresario Ivan Ackery. In May 1952, Ackery dutifully brought Cooper to the Penthouse one night along with boxer Max Baer, who also happened to be visiting the city.

Baer had been a one-time heavyweight champion of the world in 1934, and despite his aggressive strength as a boxer, he was known as a gentle giant out of the ring. Jimmy Filippone was delighted to meet Baer and, in turn, Joe entertained Cooper. On a copy of a photograph taken at the Penthouse that evening, the inscription reads, "To my pal Joe, I am happy Gary Cooper held you because you're a killer with a right hand. Your pal, Max Baer." Baer had earned a reputation as a "killer" in the ring after a notorious fight with Frankie Campbell, who died the next day from his injuries.

The daily newspapers' social pages regularly

made mention of which entertainers and household names had been in the Penthouse the night before. The newspaper writers themselves made a habit of drinking there, handing in hung-over copy on slow news days. Joe might have been accused of being fascinated with celebrities, who were certainly good for business. But it went deeper than that. "Joe was more at home with entertainers and celebrities because he was one himself," recalled Ross. "He knew everybody in town, and I think he felt more at home with show business people than some of the stuffed shirts that were in Vancouver at the time. I suppose we all did."

In town to negotiate the sale of his yacht, Errol Flynn stopped in at the Penthouse in October 1959. He'd been in town for the better part of a week charming admirers and reporters alike. Flynn said, in what would be his last interview, of his Vancouver stay, "I love this town. The people. The mountains. The sea—I've traveled a lot, and I've lived and loved a lot—that's what I'm expected to say isn't it? But I've seldom found a country as magnificent as this. It would be a wonderful place to die."[16] With those ominous words, a lifetime of wicked ways caught up with Flynn when he passed away the next day at a Vancouver West End apartment on Burnaby Street at the age of fifty.

The Penthouse remained a "bottle club" without a liquor licence, forcing patrons to hide their liquor. Regular return customers had their bottles numbered and hidden behind counters to avoid confiscation during surprise visits by the police dry squad that continued to target the Penthouse.

Boxer Sugar Ray Robinson with Ross.

Mac Colville, Ross, Maurice "the Rocket" Richard, and Joe, late 1950s.

Mickey (front, left) and Joe (standing, third from left) having fun with friends, c. 1950s.

"The police were in two or three times a week," remembered Ross Filippone. "Not just one or two guys—more like twenty of them at a time. We used to have spotters on the roof. You couldn't miss five or six police cars coming down the street. We'd press a buzzer and tell the waiters, who [told] the customers to hide their bottles or toss them on the floor."[17] Increased outcry that police were too busy raiding nightclubs and not on the streets solving crimes coincided with a public appetite for looser liquor restrictions to offer patrons more than the dreary beer parlours. Joe capitalized on this by taking the opportunity to form the BC Cabaret Owners' Association. As president, he lobbied successfully in support of a June 1952 provincial plebiscite that allowed liquor in licenced establishments. More British Columbians voted in support of relaxing liquor laws than for daylight savings time, the other proposition on the plebiscite.

It was the right place but not yet the right time for the Penthouse. While the vote was successful, and other establishments were granted licences for their cocktail bars, the Filippones' applications were denied for another fifteen years, and all the while the liquor raids continued.

"They never gave us a liquor licence, but we didn't give a damn," said Ross. "We'd had [customers] lined up and down the street. We couldn't make any more money if we had a liquor licence. We were getting $5.95 admission at the door and selling [soft drink] mix at fifty cents a bottle—$600 [of mix] only cost [us] fifty dollars. You don't make that with booze!"

At seventy-two years of age, Grant MacDonald still cuts a burly figure at six feet, four inches tall, and while he's been retired from the department for twenty years, it's still easy to picture him in a Vancouver police uniform. Despite a relaxed demeanour and sense of humour, he strikes you as a man you would not have wanted to be on the wrong side of. MacDonald joined the Vancouver Police Department at the age of twenty-four and likely epitomized what one current member

Joe and Shirley ham it up with friends including Bernie Roop on upright bass, c. 1950s.

says was the main requirement to join the VPD in the old days: "being big, tough, and Scottish."

I worked the Hastings Street beat in the mid-to late-'60s, and every Friday or Saturday they'd pull a few of us off various beats to do liquor raids. You'd do a tour of the bottle clubs. You had to go to the Penthouse. I don't think I ever seized a bottle in all those raids. Even if I did find something by this point, you were rarely charging people. You'd go into a club and find a bottle on the floor and ask the guy next to it if it was his. He might say, "Yeah, it is!" And I'd ask him, "Are you sure? I don't think it is. You know it's a fifty-dollar fine that you have to pay immediately," and he'd suddenly change his mind and say, "Oh, I've never seen that before in my life!"

It became a waste of time. We only really charged people as a tool, when we needed to get somebody out of there or charge some of the characters on Hastings Street who we were already dealing with. But overall, especially when you consider they were pulling all of us from real work on other beats, the raids were a waste of time.

Grant MacDonald, 2012. Photo: Rebecca Blissett.

Police were not the only threat to the nightclub

business in the 1960s. Their customers were going out less, preferring to stay home and stare at the flickering black-and-white shadows on television. "When you stay at home and watch the *Ed Sullivan Show*, seeing the most amazing shows for free, we had to give [people] something they hadn't seen before," said Ross, "something that they couldn't get at home."

To lure the gin-and-sin generation back to the Penthouse, the Filippones went from booking jazz bands and stand-up comedians to presenting elaborate stage shows of chorus girls wearing pasties and G-strings like those that Joe and Ross had seen on their trips to Las Vegas. And as time went by, burlesque and go-go dancing girls progressed to acts with increasingly risqué "exotic dancing."

In the beginning, the girls were only topless. In 1967, Dee Dee Special, an East Coast striptease dancer, first played the Gold Room at the Penthouse, bumping in time to a nine-piece jazz orchestra. Burlesque dancers such as Tempest Storm and Miss Lovie began to acquire celebrity status in the Penthouse's "World of Girls," and the club became a premiere stop for a circuit of burlesque entertainers.

The party at the Penthouse continued through the 1960s. Every night, the Cadillacs lined up outside, chrome sparkling on the street that never slept, with Diamond Cabs three-deep, dropping off and picking up both men and women alike. Inside, the club was full and there was lively music; patrons drank, laughed, and whispered, canoodling at corner tables, as striptease dancers, singers, emcees, and comics

IV. LIFE IS A CABARET

Penny Marks in the dressing room at the Cave, early 1960s.

Ross with Victor Borge, 1950.

Ross with football player Jackie Parker, 1950s.

Jim Backus, one of the club's glamorous dancers, and Ross, 1968.

in a variety-style revue show performed. Just about everyone had a cigarette in hand, and a blue haze of tobacco smoke coiled and drifted above the seductive tinkling of a cocktail piano. Husbands brought their wives—or somebody else's—to the bar with the growing reputation. Young couples came in to spot the who's-who of visiting celebrities that might show up on any given night to mix with local politicians, lawyers, judges, labour leaders, stockbrokers, businessmen, and sports figures, in addition to the hustlers, cheats, bad girls, or anyone else who paid the $2.50 cover. All were welcome. The Filippones had come a long way from the coal mines of Vancouver Island.

If you drove down Seymour Street at night, Ross Filippone seemed a permanent fixture at the front door—dressed in a tuxedo. "I wore a tux for thirty-five years. When I was in the club, I had my tux. If I was coming from somewhere else and couldn't stop in at home to change, I had an extra one at the Penthouse office, and I'd change before I [went to work]." Ross kept a close watch over the whole operation. While Joe and Mickey were the convivial hosts, Ross's eye for the business aspects of the club led some people to regard him as cold. "I didn't like Ross," says Edna Randle. "If he saw something or someone he didn't like, he really glared at them."

Joe, on the other hand, was the leader of the family and fit the popular conception of a nightclub owner perfectly. It was as if central casting had created him. With a twinkle in his eye and an unruly head of hair

Joe and Tony Pisani (next to Joe) are greeted by management at Caesar's Palace in Las Vegas, c. 1970s, on a talent-scouting trip.

that had been grey for years, he would move about the club giving everyone a triple greeting, saying everything three times: "How are ya, how are ya, how are ya?" or "Whaddya hear, whaddya hear, whaddya hear?" in a voice that *Vancouver Sun* columnist Denny Boyd described as having "the texture of an old army blanket … He wasn't much more than five feet tall and layered his dumpy little body with a combination of

Jimmy, Max Baer, Joe, and
Ross, 1952.

checked suits, striped shirts, and flowered ties that
made him look like a ransacked closet."[18]

Joe was always selling: "You gotta see this next act.
This girl can really play the violin. She could be in the
symphony. No, I'm serious," or bending a customer's
ear chatting about his family, the house next door, or
his mother.

Jimmy remained behind the scenes, running the
Diamond Cab business, and was less well-known to

Mickey (left), Victor Borge, and Sandy DeSantis at the Penthouse, late 1950s.

the public. "It's funny that some people thought there were only three brothers," says Jimmy's daughter, JoAnne Filippone. "My father was a quiet guy, and sometimes people mistook his quiet nature, but I suppose anybody would be considered less flashy in comparison to the other three—especially Joe and Mickey! [Jimmy] was more at home with the blue-collar people, talking with the beer delivery guys and

Penny and Ross Filippone, late 1960s.

Ross (left) and Joe with their mother Maria Rosa.

maintenance guys he always dealt with."

Mickey Filippone took after Ross's sharper style. Always dressed in a coloured pinstripe suit, he seemed to be the living reincarnation of Nathan Detroit. Shaking hands and greeting customers as maître d'— without the responsibility for the paperwork details of the business that Joe and Ross covered—he was left to socialize and interact with customers. Mickey had the liveliest sense of humour in the family. He always had a joke or a funny story, and many nightclub patrons liked Mickey the best among the Filippone brothers.

Penny Marks was a pretty, young, short-haired blonde dancer at the Cave who immigrated to Canada from England in 1960. Despite the rules preventing dancers from fraternizing with customers, she caught Ross Filippone's eye one night, and they later met at the Penthouse, where many of the city's exotic dancers dropped by after their shows. "My dancer friends told me to forget him as he was 'part of the mafia,' but they had no proof [that] he was a gangster. It just seemed they said it because he was Italian and ran a club," she recalls.

Despite the fifteen-year age difference—Ross was thirty-seven and she was twenty-two—the pair began to date. "It wasn't easy. Men were forbidden at my all-girls rooming apartment, and Ross still lived with his mother in the house next door to the Penthouse, and he didn't want to have to run the gauntlet sneaking me in! I fell very much in love with Ross, but we had to meet in hotels!"

After dating a for few months, Ross asked her to

join him at a family barbecue. Penny, who was from a prim British background, was still getting used to living in Canada, and the barbecue gave her a fish-out-of-water experience at her first encounter with a large Italian family. "It was a warm summer evening," she remembers.

In July 1961, Ross gave Penny a one-and-a-half-carat engagement ring. *Vancouver Sun* columnist and friend

We went into the house next door to the Penthouse through a side door and into a huge kitchen with a courtyard out back. There seemed to be so many people and children all talking loudly and staring at me as I was introduced to Ross's brothers and sister, cousins, and all their spouses and children.

Everyone seemed to talk at once, mostly in English but also in pidgin Italian. Ross's mother Maria—"Nana," they called her—kept saying "*mangia, mangia*" and bustling about back and forth from the kitchen where pasta was boiling. There were huge bowls of fresh peas and fava beans, enormous loaves of crusty brown bread, bottles of homemade red wine, along with water and milk on the table. Nana came out with a platter of cooked meats, then a tomato and onion salad, then another green salad with oil and vinegar dressing. A platter of fresh peaches and nectarines showed up delivered by friends from the Okanagan, and lastly, at the end of the table, was my pathetic little angel food cake that I brought to contribute! Nana only finally sat down and ate while everyone else was eating dessert. Nana's English was minimal, and she spoke in a strong Italian accent. She sat with me and just said, "So, you lika my boy? He's a good boy," while smiling at me in a friendly way.

of the Filippones Jack Wasserman wrote in his talk-of-the-town column, "Showgirl Penny Marks is sporting such a big diamond ring that she can barely lift her hand." Their wedding was a decidedly Filippone affair. With few close friends or family in Vancouver, the bride was almost a spectator at her own wedding. The guests were a broad mix of Vancouver's who's-who, along with many old family friends, cousins,

Maria "Nana" Filippone's recipe, handed down to Penny, as served at family dinners.

Nana's Spaghetti & Meatballs

Tomato Sauce:
4 tbsp olive oil
1 large onion, finely chopped
2 stalks celery, chopped
3 garlic cloves, finely chopped
3 tbsp tomato paste
1 large can whole tomatoes
salt to taste
pepper to taste
3 tbsp chopped parsley
1 tsp dried oregano
½ tsp dried red pepper flakes

In a heavy saucepan on medium, heat oil. Add onions, celery, and garlic and sauté for about 5 minutes, stirring occasionally, until soft. Push vegetables to one side of the pan to make a space to add the tomato paste. Stir with a wooden spoon until it sizzles, then stir into vegetables. Tip the can of tomatoes into a bowl and break up with your fingers, then add to pan. Add ½ cup water to tomato can, swirl around, and add to pan. Season with salt and pepper, add parsley, oregano, and red pepper flakes, and bring to a boil. Reduce heat and simmer for about 30 minutes.

Meatballs:
1 lb (450 g) organic ground pork
½ lb (225 g) organic ground beef
salt to taste
pepper to taste
1 tsp dried oregano
3 tbsp chopped parsley
1 egg, beaten
½ cup fine breadcrumbs

Combine all ingredients by hand and form into meatballs about the size of golf balls. Carefully drop them into the simmering tomato sauce, ensuring that they are covered in sauce. Cover pan and cook for about 40 minutes.

Spaghetti:
1 tsp salt
1 lb (450 g) dried spaghetti
Fresh Parmesan cheese

Bring a large pot of water to a boil. Add salt and spaghetti and cook for about 10 minutes until al dente. Drain, then add to a large serving platter. Arrange meatballs and sauce on top but serve extra sauce on the side. Grate fresh Parmesan cheese on top and serve.

and significant members of the Italian community. Penny's old boss Ken Stauffer, manager at the Cave, gave her away at a packed wedding at Holy Rosary Cathedral (Marks, an Episcopalian, had converted to Catholicism). At a reception after the wedding, telegrams from her family in England wishing her well were read aloud. "A couple of them ended with 'love from all the *gang*,'" she laughs, remembering that this drew surprised looks from "some of the Italians, who had a different understanding of the word!"

Within a couple of years, Ross and Penny had two sons, Joey and Danny, and then a daughter named Maria. When she got married, Penny quit her life as a showgirl; the duties of taking care of three small children became her full-time job. Ross's work hours at the Penthouse continued to be late and long, and this put inevitable strains on the marriage. "We never used to stop," said Ross. "I used to work until six in the morning. I'd get up a noon and get things organized, have dinner, have a couple of hours sleep, then head back at ten at night."

In the autumn of 1968, the Penthouse finally got its liquor licence. Joe was ecstatic. After twenty years, the dry squad raids were finally over. The Filippones closed the club briefly to renovate, then reopened on December 15, 1968 as the New Penthouse. *Vancouver Sun* Leisure Section editor Alex MacGillivray heralded the opening in his column, noting that "the city's oldest stationary funhouse appears to be going all out in an honest try now that it has a new interior and that all-important liquor licence from Victoria. Creating

the right image is important to the Filippones because they realize that they are just one of about twenty-five city cabarets and that the competition is rough for the customer's dollar. But they do have an advantage—they've outlasted just about everybody and the club is well known."

An accompanying photo shows brothers Joe, Mickey, and Ross behind a well-stocked bar with liquor now right out in the open. Mickey smiles, standing behind a bartender, while Joe looks curiously at a liquor bottle

Ross with Penthouse wait staff. Photo: *Vancouver Sun* Archives

Joe, Mickey, and Ross get the bar ready, after finally getting a license, 1968. Photo: *Vancouver Sun* Archives.

like it's the first he's ever seen. Behind them, Ross playfully holds his hands to his ears, perhaps thinking of the ringing of the cash register. The Penthouse had reached the age of twenty-one, and it was finally legal. The Filippones saw this as a great start to a new decade, and they looked forward to the promise of 1970s.

By the beginning of the 1970s, the golden age of Vegas, which the Penthouse had mirrored, was fading. The black-and-white 1960s of men stepping out of Cadillacs in tuxes with cummerbunds accompanied by women in satin dresses with mink stoles were gone; now, businessmen in orange-and-brown checkerboard slacks and wide, patterned ties parked their Fleetwood Broughams in front of the club. The music had changed too. There was less bebop jazz and more bump-and-grind as dancers stripped to songs such as "Pass the Hatchet Part II" by Roger & the Gypsies. If the Penthouse of the 1950s and '60s was a restrained cocktail party, the changing times brought an anything-goes ambience where, in fact, everything went.

When the *Vancouver Sun* first wrote about Philliponi's new Eagle Time building in the 1940s, Joe was quoted as saying: "By maintaining always cordial relations with the public, we are able to develop our business continually, and here in this new plant we have facilities that will enable us to give even better service." Thirty years later, the owners of the Penthouse had found themselves serving the public in a different way.

While prostitution in the Downtown Eastside of Vancouver had long been a problem, the higher end call-girl business generally didn't take place on the streets but in hotels and nightclubs. While it was not the only club in which this occurred, the Penthouse had become a flourishing focal point of high-class prostitution in Vancouver at night. This wasn't a totally new development, but one that had grown over time.

V. DOLLARS AND SEX

Early 1970s Penthouse exterior.

Mid-1970s Penthouse ad.

Edna Randle remembers regularly seeing a woman named "Madame Sandra" in the club, even in the late 1950s. "She had all these beautiful girls around her. Maybe I just didn't get it, but then I figured the reason they called her 'Madame' was because she was French!"

In a *Vancouver Sun* article published in December 1977, columnist Allan Fotheringham remarked, "The hooker shop known as the Penthouse has been existing for decades. It has been known as one of the landmarks of the town, a minor league equivalent of the Eiffel Tower and the Empire State building."[19] Certainly by the early 1970s, the club was often home to more than a hundred prostitutes who used it as their workplace. Saxophonist Dave Davies, who performed at the Penthouse in the early '70s, observed that, "there were resident hookers. Some of [them] were just goddesses. They were just stunning women. Beautiful women. Real style, class, dressed to the nines, cultured women."[20]

Prostitution wasn't a public nuisance when it was kept indoors and off the streets, but it was still a crime. Retired Constable Vern Campbell spent eight months on Vancouver's vice squad in 1973. An affable, well-spoken Vancouver East Ender, Campbell still recalls the nights when he had to pose undercover as a john. "I joined the VPD when I was pretty young. I'd never been to the Penthouse before. The first time I ever went in there, I was undercover. Typically, your routine was, you'd go in, sit down, have a drink, and really just wait for the solicitation to take place. The older vice-squad

Exotic dancers on stage.

Detective George Barclay and Constable Vern Campbell escorting a suspect under arrest, 1970s. Photo courtesy of Vern Campbell.

guys were a lot better at tricking the hookers than I was. Those girls spotted me as a cop a mile away," Campbell laughs.

After meeting a prostitute and arranging a price, Campbell would suggest that they leave go to his car or a nearby hotel. A pick-up team from the squad would be in position outside, watching and waiting for the undercover constable to come out. "They'd usually let you walk a block away to distance yourself from the club before they stepped out to make an arrest. Sometimes, if you were working with some asshole pranksters they'd make you sweat, they would wait awhile until it looked like the girl was about to get too friendly before they'd come out and make the arrest. The pick-up team guys would never acknowledge that they knew you, so you just pretended to be an embarrassed john on a night out from the wife. The girls never actually knew who you were until they saw you in court."

For vice-squad police, too many nights at the Penthouse tended to jeopardize their undercover abilities. For Detective George Barclay, who worked undercover in 1975, it once produced a humorous result. "I remember walking down Granville street with my wife one night. We were headed to the Orpheum. A woman tapped my wife on the shoulder as she passed and whispered to her, 'He's a policeman!' My wife told me this, and I turned around and recognized one of the regular Penthouse hookers I'd arrested. I had to explain that the girl thought my wife was a hooker and was trying to warn her. We had a good laugh about that."

Police also found the prostitutes great sources of information about the men they did business with, and they often told police about what they'd overheard or had been bragged to about, including who'd been behind a robbery, stock tips, and as-yet-unannounced cabinet-ministry shuffles in Victoria. For police officers like Grant MacDonald, who were able to establish a friendly rapport with some of them, these women became informants.

One night, we answered a dispatch call at about three a.m. from a woman who'd been attacked on her front steps going into her West End apartment. While getting her name, address, occupation, etc., she tells us she's a working girl. I think she figured that we wouldn't take a statement from a hooker seriously, but we ended up catching the guy. We became social with her, seeing her around the Penthouse, and she'd tell us if pimps were trying to move in or trying to hustle any of the girls. It was interesting because she was a nice looking young lady that just had a dollar figure in her mind that once she hit it she was out. She wasn't abused or anything typical. Her job was never an issue to her, it's just what she did for a living.

With the liquor raids over, MacDonald and his partner were shifted to a special plainclothes squad in the early 1970s. They continued their former rounds but now dropped in every night at the Penthouse as part of an intelligence detail to observe the comings and goings of figures in the Vancouver underworld.

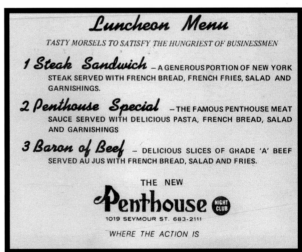

"My liver still shudders to think about those days," MacDonald laughs. "You couldn't just stand with your thumb up your ass and hope to see or overhear something. They knew us as police, but you still needed to ingratiate yourself by buying a drink and hanging out. Joe would always stop me when I came in. 'Hey Grant, Grant! How are ya? You alone or by

Mickey, Maria Rosa, Joe, and Jimmy in the 1970s.

yourself tonight?' He thought that was the funniest line ever. The Filippones were all nice guys—I liked them all. But they were a little nervous when we came in and would stand near us to keep an eye on us," says MacDonald. It wasn't as though the Filippones didn't like the police, they just felt better when they weren't around. "One night, when we were in plainclothes there, Joe was busy talking to my partner when this gorgeous young lady starts chatting me up. One thing leads to another, and she asks me what I do for a living. I told her I worked for the city," MacDonald chuckles. "She eventually asks me if I'd like to go out. I said, 'I'd love to go out with a girl as pretty as you, but I can't.' She said 'Why not?' and I told her, 'Because I'm a policeman.' She was shocked I'd told her up front, and thanked me profusely for not running her in. That got around the room pretty quick that I wasn't there to bust them. The main reason we were there was to go in and check around the upstairs lounge."

While the main floor Gold Room functioned as the lounge and main stage for shows, the upstairs contained the Steak Loft restaurant and a front-room lounge. Where Edna Randle had seen Oscar Peterson and Jack Teagarden years before was now a seedy rogue's gallery of criminals who held court under increasing police scrutiny.

John Kenneth Eccles had already been arrested for drug trafficking, heroin and marijuana possession, assault, and theft, and he was known to police as one of the city's main heroin and cocaine dealers. He had a pilot's licence, and with his criminal connections in the United States, police had investigated him for flying cross-border drug shipments. A tall, thin man with long hair, Eccles sped through the city streets in his 1958 Corvette, often with his beautiful nineteen-year-old wife Sunshine, a flowers-in-her-hair hippie girl, who police also believed prostituted for him. "The question in every police officer's mind that met her was, 'What is she doing with *him*?'" MacDonald says. "We all concluded that he had lots of money and a good supply of drugs."

Then there was Eccles' notorious friend Eddie Cheese. In August 1971, police raided his apartment. Cheese had outstanding warrants in Montreal, but because the plainclothes policemen had failed to properly identify themselves when they entered the apartment, the charges were dismissed. Eccles was awarded damages, as the police were found to have technically trespassed. The case was precedent-setting and was appealed by the Crown up to the Supreme Court of Canada. Cheese was delighted that he'd won the case, and had been so bothersome to the police without ever leaving home.

"Eccles wasn't a likeable guy," says MacDonald. "In my thirty years in the force, I could count on one hand the number of guys it became personal to catch. With Eccles, you could get a rise out of him to talk to you, but Eddie Cheese didn't show any emotion."

Along with Eccles and Cheese in the upstairs Penthouse lounge, "There was Paul Gray, who was involved importing drugs, and Dennis Walton who had a patch over one eye," MacDonald recalls.

Exotic dancer on stage, c. 1970s.

Penthouse dancer on stage, 1973.

"The Levinson brothers—Peter and Paul—were international jewel thieves, some of the best in the world, who'd gone through Europe like a dose of salts and pulled jobs here in Vancouver, too. There was Al Oda, a Japanese guy who looked like Oddjob from the James Bond movie. We were in there to see who was sitting with who. Later on down the line, you'd compare notes if something went down. 'Okay, on that night I saw the two of them together, so that makes sense'—that sort of thing."

If a customer came to the Penthouse to spend money, who were the Filippones to ask if he had an arrest record? Even if he was a little shady, he might open his wallet and buy rounds all night for a whole table. As for the prostitutes, the Filippone brothers tended to look the other way. "We weren't denying there were hookers in the club. We didn't show any dislike or encouragement to them. We didn't treat them any differently than regular customers," Ross Filippone later recalled. "We didn't want them to table hop. But if a guy wanted to buy a girl a drink, that was his business."

And it was clear they were good for business. In addition to bringing in customers to see the shows, the prostitutes paid the three-dollar cover charge just as regular customers did, and paid again when they returned from turning a trick.

So the Penthouse patrons, honest and dishonest, blended together on any given evening. Club owners and musicians mingled with cabinet ministers and newspaper editors. Off-duty policemen chatted with

Exotic dancer Danielle Dean, the "Queen of the Champagne Glass," in the Green Room.

Toni Pisani with Dee Dee Special in the early 1970s.

safe-crackers, and corporation presidents drank with short-order cooks. For "girl watchers," there was no reason to go to the beach. With the club full of hookers, eggheads met redheads as all kinds of cheating husbands, stockbrokers, school principals, celebrities, PTA presidents, and gamblers shared tables—and the Vancouver police undercover teams surveyed it all.

New family members were now employed at the Penthouse as well. Mickey's twenty-year-old daughter Rose began to work in the ticket cashier's office in 1974, and Jimmy's daughter JoAnne, when still a teenager, began work as a cigarette girl on weekends. "It was like how you used to see it in the movies, with a girl holding out a little tray. I sold cigarettes, cigars, gum, and lifesavers," says JoAnne. "It was great money for a kid my age!" Being involved in the family business made her privy to an adult realm that was the envy of many of her friends.

JoAnne remembers watching emcee Tony Pisani— billed as the Mario Lanza of Vancouver—open the evening's entertainment with a few songs (including his rendition of Al Martino's "Spanish Eyes," featuring a ribald lyrical amendment to "Spanish Flies"), then introduce Danielle Dean, who danced inside a larger-than-life-size champagne glass filled with warm, bubbling, tinted water. "It was like another world. There was glamour and glitz and high rollers and celebrities. If there were hoodlums there, I couldn't tell [who they were], everybody was so well dressed! And while I knew there was an element of call girls there, I never felt threatened or unsafe; they and the dancers were beautiful. As a young adolescent girl, it was an amazing world to watch. Backstage, I got to meet these incredible burlesque stars with their costumes, feathers, and sequins—just beautifully adorned. They were great shows."

The Penthouse continued to be "home" to an array of visiting actors and entertainers, from Lee Marvin to Ed Asner. Vegas comedians such as Jack E. Leonard and Frank Gorshin performed or came to the Steak Loft. "Bombshell" actresses Jayne Mansfield and Jane Russell dropped in, and musicians ranging from jazz stars Louis Prima and Woody Herman to 1970s rock bands like Fleetwood Mac and Led Zeppelin came in after their own shows when in town.

"My partner and I stopped into the Penthouse in uniform one night when the Boston Bruins were in town," says Grant MacDonald. "Don Cherry and two or three other players were seated right down at the front watching the dancers—they were pretty drunk. We were standing at the back of the bar just having a look around. Cherry sees us, and starts going into his act. 'Hey, check out the monkeys at the back.' The place went dead still. I saw Joe was worried. Cherry kept acting like a big shot. You can put up with a bit of it if it's funny, but eventually it can get to the point where it's abusive. I walked down to him and very quietly told him, 'You know you can go to jail in this town?' That was the end of it. He never said another word. He had a lot more to lose than I did!"

"The parties were *unbelievable*," says Al Abraham. The amicable East Ender became a Penthouse regular

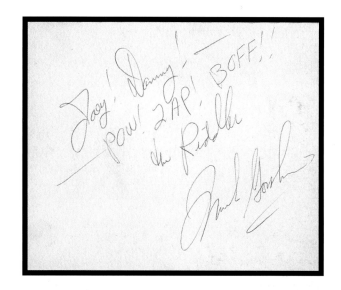

Frank Gorshin (second from left) with Ross (left) and Mickey (far right) and an unidentified friend.

The Ladybirds, billed as the world's first all-girl topless band, performed at the Penthouse in the early 1970s.

when in his twenties and fell in socially with Eccles and his crew, drinking and hanging out with some of the very same people that MacDonald was keeping an eye on. "The years 1969 to 1975 was the greatest time ever—the money was really flowing. To spend a grand on a Friday night, which was a lot of money back then, was nothing to these guys, and the Penthouse was the spot. Everybody went there. We always hung out upstairs. They had great food up at the Steak Loft— and the place was full of rounders." It's a term that Abraham says with relish and uses frequently when talking about the old days.

A rounder was someone who was street-wise. They'd literally 'been around.' They learned everything from the curb. Maybe they'd done a little time for something—real characters. You don't see guys like that now. You see Hells Angels around today; those guys are nothing compared to back then. A lot of guys now are fringe—they try to act tough, but those were the real deal, those guys were connected. Back then, when you wanted to know something, you went to certain guys. One year some thieves broke into Hunter's Sporting Goods up on Kingsway, and they got all their guns stolen—it was a big deal. The police had something on Eccles and they went to him. He had nothing to do with it, but he made some inquiries on the street and got all the guns back. They even anonymously got delivered right to the police station— and whatever they had on Eccles got forgotten!

Eccles and Cheese were nice guys, actually. They just didn't care about living straight. They had a few rackets going on and suitcases of money to show for it. I remember they had a guy named Baxter who would dope horses to fix races out at the track. That's one thing I learned from those days. Any time there's money involved, it's rigged. Everything's rigged! I don't know one thing that ain't.

Abraham's eyes light up and he smiles as he remembers the coterie of characters around the bar in the early '70s.

There was a black guy named Shoe Polish, and another guy named Perfume Jack, who was a fence. Shoulders Levy was another—he had watches in his coat, and he went around to clubs and sold them. There was a guy called Cowboy John, who was always in Western clothing, and another guy, the head of a big construction firm, who'd drink at the bar wearing just a kimono while he kept a cab running, ready to take him home. I'm not kidding!

After a night at the Penthouse, we'd pile in my car, a '72 Cadillac Eldorado. I'd put on Al Green or "The Love I Lost" by Harold Melvin & the Blue Notes and we'd roar up at three a.m. to my friend Brown Bear's 'booze can' [private after-hours club] he ran out of a house on 14th and Oak. The bar was in the kitchen. They had eighteen couches in the living room, a pool table in the basement, and a card game going upstairs. Eccles would get on the phone, ten or fifteen hookers would show up, and we'd keep the party going. It was unbelievable! I'd leave around seven in the morning and get a couple of hours sleep before I went back to my day job. I don't know how I did it!

As much as Abraham enjoyed the parties and was a welcome regular, he tried to keep his distance from Eccles and his cohorts. "I gambled with them and did some driving, but I stayed out of the serious stuff. I didn't need to go to jail for twenty years just because I liked driving a new car every year," he says. Abraham remembers the regular prostitutes at the Penthouse well, noting that a lot of them lived at the Century Plaza Hotel on Burrard Street just blocks away from the Penthouse.

Late at night we'd hear the stories. One girl, Joan, would meet a logger who came into town every few months. He'd want to go down to Industrial Avenue at night when nobody was around, and Joan would smack him on the ass with a tire iron. Right there, naked, in the middle of the street! There was another guy, some lawyer or stockbroker or something, and she used to put a towel over his knob and jump all over him in her high heels. Unbelievable! They were just such crazy stories, and everybody at the party would be laughing, hearing this shop talk.

A lot of broads are attracted to that lifestyle, too—guys spend a lot of money on them. Truth be told from what I saw, a lot of men would want the same woman over and over again. I still know some of the women. They have families now, but they still take their regular customers from the old days. It's hard to say no to that cash.

Abraham isn't naming names—but it does give one pause to think of some Vancouver housewives' hidden pasts.

Meanwhile, Diamond Cabs was still going strong, and although not one of the biggest cab companies in the city, it was certainly one of the most memorable to work for. "They had a midget dispatcher in the office, along with Jimmy Filippone who ran the cab company," recalls Bob Burrows. In the early 1970s, Burrows was "just another longhair" in his twenties bumming around Vancouver's counterculture, when he arrived at Diamond Cabs looking for a job.

"I got fired by Yellow Cab because I wouldn't cut my hair," he says. "So I went to Joe and asked him for a job. He thought it was the funniest thing in the world that I'd been fired for not cutting my hair, and on that basis alone seemed to hire me. Joe was always really good to me. But he'd always try to buy you a drink after he paid you, then hope you'd stay and drink your wages down. With a few of the older drivers, that seemed to work.

"Ross was all business, and I never really talked with him. But I really liked Mickey," Burrows continues. "When that *Goodfellas* movie came out I kept thinking, when I saw Joe Pesci's character, that was Mickey! He wasn't violent like that, it was just the quick-talking, the sense of humour. He was a great guy, with his cigars and a big diamond ring and his suits."

Burrows also remembers the patrons that he drove to or took home from the club. "My customers were gangsters, prostitutes, judges, or lawyers. Joe was

always curious who I drove or if they'd said anything to me or I overheard anything. There was a hooker there who I drove home almost every night, until her pimp beat her up and near crippled her. I never saw her after that. One Christmas Eve, it was snowing like hell, and I took home this drunken businessman. He wanted to stop off at Forest Lawn Cemetery in Burnaby and scream and swear at his father's grave before I took him home. It was absolutely crazy. One after another like that."

Burrows, who was later active in the Vancouver nightclub business for forty years and became particularly well-known in the 1980s and '90s for booking clubs including the Town Pump, Richard's on Richards, and Venue, got his start in the business while still a Diamond Cabs driver.

Around the time I was working [as a cab driver], I took over this place in the back of the Shanghai Junk nightclub in Chinatown that we called the Pink Parlour. It was a real hippie palace—bead curtains and big pillows—that we ran as an after-hours booze can with music. Joe heard about it and wanted to see what I was doing. He was curious if he was missing out on anything. One night, he came in with a few friends—these tough Italian bruisers in their suits who stuck out like crazy. The place was full of body painted hippies drinking and doing LSD. Everybody was fucked up in there, but it looked lively! We had no liquor or business licence. Joe just thought it was great. "Hey, hey, you're doing a good job, Bob! It's nice to see a young kid being enterprising and getting a leg up in the world."

In July 1974, Don Winterton was named new chief constable of the Vancouver Police Department.[22] Described as a "squeaky clean guy with a new broom," he'd been involved with prostitution crackdown strategies for years.[23] While a number of city nightclubs and hotel lounges were used as working areas by prostitutes, the Penthouse, after years of indifference, was suddenly targeted. The reasons for this have remained a cause for speculation. But Winterton wished to demonstrate his administration's dedication to ridding Vancouver of prostitutes once and for all, and to this end, he appointed Inspector John Samuel Victor "Vic" Lake as the new head of the vice squad.

Lake joined the city police in 1946. His first contact with the Penthouse wasn't until 1966, when he'd been posted to the liquor squad and took part in some of the "bottle raids" before the Penthouse got its licence. He knew all the tricks; he knew, for example, that some of his supervisors, after the drama of a raid was over, would go up to Joe's office for a drink before they left. Joe later stated that Lake had a personal vendetta against him, telling Jack Wasserman on the CBC television show *Hourglass* that Lake would sit in the bar out of uniform, wait until a patron at a nearby table produced a bottle, and catch them in the act. While Lake publicly denied any personal animosity toward the Filippones, he did undertake his new task with unexpected zeal.

Like Winterton, Lake had strong attitudes about prostitutes. "Vic was a real straight arrow—maybe one of the straightest guys on the force then," recalls retired

VI.
SET 'EM UP [21]

Mickey, unknown, Joe, Jimmy, Dee Dee Special, legendary Montreal Canadien Bernie "Boom Boom" Geoffrion, and Ross at the club, mid-1970s.

Penthouse 'hangout for Mafia'

By CHUCK POULSEN

↳ ≠ 11-76

The Penthouse Cabaret was a meeting place for the kingpins of the "local Mafia," Vancouver vice squad detective Norman Elliott said in County Court Friday.

Elliot said that during an early-morning conversation at the club, one of the defendants in the Penthouse prostitution trial, Joe Philliponi, confirmed that a Mafia meeting was taking place.

"I said (to Philliponi) that it looked like a gathering of the local Mafia and he went on to say that I was right . . .," said Elliot.

"He said they were all up there, except their leader."

Elliot said Philliponi identified the lead-er as a John Eccles, whom Elliot has named several times in his testimony as a frequent visitor to the cabaret.

Elliot, who spent several months investigating the club in 1975, added that Philliponi told him that Eccles' "right-hand man" (later named as a Wayne Murray) was at the meeting along with "most of his cohorts."

Elliot said Philliponi also mentioned the names of two others who were attending the meeting — a Les Stork and a Tony Gardner — and that both of them had once attempted to take over the club.

"Joe said that at one time not long ago 'those two bastards tried to take over the club . . . tried to tell me which girls were to work out of here and which girls were to be banned. But there was no way they were going to get away with that'."

While Judge William Trainor ruled that the earlier part of the conversation was the club. On several occasions he observed Ross Filippone, the club's unofficial book-keeper, "putting bundles of money into a briefcase."

Asked Chamberlain: "You have certain views about the Filippones don't you? You think they're pimps, don't you?"

Elliot: "Yes, I do."

The detective conceded that he drank regularly at the club and on one night consumed 12 drinks.

He also said that on one occasion he went out for dinner with one of the Pent-house's dancers, but denied Chamber-lain's suggestion that he had bought two bottles of champagne that night and had them brought to his table before leaving.

Chamberlain: "You said to Joe that you'd really like to meet that dancer, didn't you?"

Elliot: "No."

Chamberlain: "You were really enam-

Chief Constable Don Winterton. Photo courtesy of the Vancouver Police Museum.

constable Vern Campbell. "He was really into physical fitness, which wasn't that common to inspectors at the time. He was young when he was made an inspector, and I think in some cases, he rubbed a few guys in the department the wrong way."

With Lake at the helm, the vice squad launched an unprecedented investigation into the Penthouse that was kept secret from the beat cops in the area. The squad parked a camper van across the street from the club, and with a hidden camera, photographed prostitutes and patrons as they entered and exited the club. They also wiretapped the Penthouse telephones.

Of key interest to Lake's task force on the Penthouse were the cover charges that the customers paid for admittance. Prostitutes who frequented the nightclub were required to pay the cover again each time they returned to the building, and they tipped the staff to get prime seating. Lake's investigation also focused on the cash advances the Penthouse made available to those wishing to use their credit cards, and the fact that the Filippones added a surcharge to each advance. That the Penthouse management was essentially allowing customers to put the costs of hiring a prostitute on their credit cards is not as peculiar as it may now seem. Before instant teller bank machines offered twenty-four-hour access, if you didn't have any cash, you had to wait until the bank opened the next day. Joe, during Lake's surveillance, was recorded colourfully commenting on these cash advances to an undercover policeman. "[You] can go into a bank and say 'Look, I've got two prostitutes outside in cab and I need $200,' and the bank clerk wouldn't care." Nevertheless, Inspector Lake and his team considered the repeat cover charges, tips, and cash advance surcharges as tantamount to profiting from prostitution.

In addition to the surveillance and wiretaps, Lake put someone on the inside. "There were taxis coming and going with girls. It was a zoo," recalls retired Constable Leslie McKellar who, at the age of twenty-one, was plucked from the police academy for her first assignment as an undercover prostitute at the Penthouse. McKellar spent four to five nights a week at the club from May to August 1975.[24] She would leave with undercover officers posing as customers looking for sex, report her findings to them, and then return to the club as if she'd left to turn a trick.

Penthouse trial told local Mafia tried takeover

By LARRY STILL

Members of the "local Mafia" have attempted to seize control of the Penthouse cabaret, it was alleged Friday in Vancouver county court.

But Joe Philliponi, senior citizen among the family partnership that has run the Seymour Street nightspot for decades, resisted the takeover bid.

The reference to the Mafia, in a local sense in no way connected with the internationally known Cosa Nostra, was made by Det. Norman Elliot.

He has testified for four days at a trial in which the principals of the Penthouse are accused of pimping and of corrupting public morals.

Elliot, who frequented the club for five months posing as a police officer looking for pimps, told Judge William Trainor that he gained the confidence of the management.

During his first three days on the witness stand, Elliot told prosecutor Roy Jaques that he had seen as many as 150 prostitutes in the club on some evenings.

Continuing his testimony Friday, Elliot said he spoke to Juan Santana, the club's bartender, on July 21, 1975, and Santana noted that Leslie Stork and Tony Gardner were on the premises.

"He said Stork was out of jail on an appeal and he considered both men very dangerous," Elliot told the court.

The detective recalled that Joe Philliponi then joined in the conversation and said: "You know at one time not too long ago those two bastards tried to take over the club."

Elliot said Philliponi added: "They tried to tell me which girls were to work out of here and which ones should be barred, but there is no way they are going to get away with that."

The detective said he then made a reference to the group of men in the club's dining room and said it looked like a gathering of the local mafia.

He said Philliponi agreed with his assessment of the group as "local Mafia," a term not intended to suggest that the real Mafia frequented the club.

All but leader at gathering

Elliot said Philliponi continued: "They're all up there but their leader."

The detective said he asked the club owner who the leader was and Philliponi said: John Eccles.

Elliot said Philliponi added: "His right hand man is there and most of his cohorts."

The witness said he asked for the name of the right-hand man and Philliponi said it was Wayne Murray.

The reference to the "local Mafia" and to Eccles and Murray was subject to an objection by defence lawyer S. R. Chamberlain.

Judge Trainor ruled that all the testimony on the "local Mafia" and Eccles and Murray was not admissible as evidence against any of the accused in the trial.

The accused are Joseph Philliponi, Ross Filippone, Domenick Filippone, Jan Sedlak, Minerva Kelly and Rose Filippone.

They and Celebrity Enterprises, the Penthouse corporation, are charged with living off the avails of prostitution and with corrupting public morals.

During cross-examination by Chamberlain, Elliot said he and an undercover team of police officers spent 11 days with a hidden camera taking photographs of all persons entering and leaving the club.

Outside the courtroom, a police officer told The Vancouver Sun that the photographic surveillance team took 700 photographs, of which only 200 are being used in the trial.

Asked who might have appeared in the pictures not used in the trial, the police officer said: "Well, let's say a blackmailer could make a fortune. There were lots of very distinguished gentlemen.'"

Police file unused photographs

The police officer said the remaining 500 photographs will not be destroyed, but will be kept on file by city police.

During his cross-examination, Chamberlain reminded Elliot that he had testified that he saw as many as 150 women and 300 men in the club on some evenings.

insisted that he repeated-the identifications he had made at the preliminary hearing and during his examination by prosecutor Roy Jaques.

During four hours of relentless questioning, Chamberlain showed that many of the identifications Elliot made at the pre-

METRO

Not a petting officer —an ex-petty officer

The coincidence seemed too improbable for George Burton to dismiss the suspicion that he was being impersonated.

And by a Vancouver city vice squad officer at that.

Burton, 64, is a former navy petty officer who works in the boiler shop at Esquimalt's HMCS dockyards.

And he reached boiling point when he read that vice squad Detective Ken Johnstone had used his name and background while investigating a prostitution case currently being heard in Vancouver county court.

Johnstone testified Friday that he posed as a chief petty officer working for the defence department in Esquimalt and used the name George Burton while negotiating last December with a woman at the Penthouse Cabaret.

"I was pretty mad," Burton said Wednesday. "I used to work with a guy named Ken Johnstone about eight years ago. His mother-in-law lived two houses down from us."

But Johnstone, the detective, said although he once worked at the naval dockyards in Esquimalt he never knew George Burton.

At least, not that George Burton.

"The George Burton I know is a city police constable," said Johnstone. "I needed a credit card in the investigation and I was given one belonging to Burton, the constable."

Johnstone also said he is a chief petty officer in the naval reserve and that he acted under cover of a defence department employee because he was familiar with the work.

Inspector Vic Lake of the vice squad called the coincidence strange and apologized to the Esquimalt dockyard worker for any embarrassment.

"Maybe we're going to have to start every trial with, 'Any similarity between these and actual persons is strictly a coincidence'," said Lake.

In the upstairs lounge, McKellar observed the Filippones' interactions with Eccles, Cheese, Oda, and their other associates. "The Filippones acted the best of friends with them," she says exasperatedly. That the management might have been especially attentive to them because they were regularly dropping hundreds of dollars at the club was of no relevance to McKellar, who still holds strong opinions about the Penthouse and the Filippones. "The Filippones [made me] automatically think of old Mafia movies—always with their cigars. I never liked Mickey. Ross was a classy guy, but I was scared of him because he was so observant and never missed a thing. I didn't like how they all catered to Eccles and those guys."

On July 10, 1975, police began monitoring the business telephone of the Penthouse and the home phone of the Filippones. On July 18, Sergeant Mike Beattie filed a report to his supervisor (the details of which are made public here for the first time), updating him on the details of the wiretap surveillance.[25] Beattie noted that several calls made on the pay telephone were regarding prostitution. In one call, a man wanted to hire two women to travel to Victoria to perform at a stag party. When the woman on the line wanted to know if there was "anything on the side" she could do, intrigued police were convinced that the Penthouse was not just a hangout but a dispatch network for prostitutes. Beattie also reported a conversation intercepted between Joe and another man detailing a business deal in excess of $1 million.[26] During the call, Joe declined the deal, but

Beattie nevertheless concluded that it was part of a loan-sharking operation he was involved in.

Police suspected that Mickey was running a bookmaking operation out of the Penthouse after overhearing various people contact him to take sports bets, usually of wagers between twenty and fifty dollars. On July 14, a man named Phil Benson called to place a bet on a horse named "Proud Bird" in the eighth race that day at Exhibition Park racetrack.[27] Whether Benson figured he had a hot tip or a good hunch is unknown, but Mickey accepted the twenty-dollar-to-win bet. Unfortunately for Benson, Proud Bird ran last in the race.[28]

"We used to bet through Mickey on Super Bowl games," Al Abraham recalls. "He'd take any bet. At his house, he'd have three or four small televisions, each showing a different sport, so he could figure out his bets. You see that all the time now in sports bars, but this was in the 1970s, and he was doing it right in his living room!"

But Lake was primarily looking for evidence that directly connected the Penthouse to the prostitutes, evidence that proved that the Filippones weren't just businessmen who ran a bar frequented by them, but were also acting as their pimps. Although the police never heard or found any evidence to support this allegation, Lake believed the Filippones were profiting financially from their presence. Beattie's report suggests another reason why the police department focused so much effort against the Penthouse—they were trying to connect the Filippones to John Eccles

'Offence' to uncover an undercover officer

By LARRY STILL

Uncovering an undercover officer can constitute an offence, a police witness said Tuesday in Vancouver county court.

Det. George Barclay, testifying in the Penthouse trial, said he once charged a prostitute with obstruction after she pointed him out as an undercover officer. The witness said the incident occurred in the Penthouse in January, 1975, prior to the period covered in the indictment before the court.

Charged with conspiring to live off the avails of prostitution and with conspiring to corrupt public morals are Joe Philliponi, Ross, Domenick and Rose Filippone, Jan Sedlak and Minerva Kelly.

The offences are alleged to have been committed at the Seymour Street night-spot between May 29 and Nov. 7, 1975.

Barclay told prosecutor Roy Jaques he visited the club in an undercover capacity on eight different occasions in the period covered by the indictment.

The detective said he dressed casually, maintained a low profile and sometimes altered his appearance by wearing glasses or a wig.

He said he was solicited in the club by women and recalled one occasion when a woman "offered me sex" for $60. He said he identified himself to the woman as a policeman.

During cross-examination, defence lawyer Russ Chamberlain suggested that Barclay's guise as the bespectacled and wigged patron was to no avail because the Penthouse management knew his true identity.

Barclay, formerly with the vice squad and now with the drug squad, agreed that he has known prostitutes all over the city since 1964.

He agreed that he had investigated the activities of prostitutes in the Marine Room of the Bayshore Inn, the Devonshire, Georgia, Hyatt Regency and Stratford hotels.

Questioned about his visits to the Penthouse prior to May 29, 1975, Barclay hesitated and said: "I thought you were trying to trick me."

Chamberlain: "I'm not going to trick you. I'm going to ask you fair questions."

The detective then agreed that he was in the Penthouse in January, 1975, and charged a girl with obstruction because she pointed him out as an undercover officer.

He denied Chamberlain's suggestion that he revealed his true identity to Joe Philliponi and Ross Filippone in January, 1975, and said he did not discuss with them the obstruction matter.

After further questions about the officer's vice squad activities, Chamberlain said: "And you still labor under the belief that they (the Penthouse management) didn't know who you were?" The witness replied: "Yes."

To further questions, Barclay admitted that some of the evidence he gave at the preliminary inquiry into the charges conflicted with the evidence he has given in the trial.

"I made a mistake," he explained at one point to Judge William Trainor.

The judge was told earlier in the trial that some male patrons, with insufficient cash to pay the $60 to $100 fee for a prostitute's services, could use their credit cards for a cash advance from the club's management.

At the hearing Tuesday, Albert Band, a security officer with the Royal Bank, identified two Chargex drafts, one for $90 and one for $72.35, which were signed by Bruce Ballantyne and deposited to the club's account.

In earlier testimony, Constable Bruce Ballantyne said he went to the Penthouse in an undercover capacity and there met a girl named Lena who told him she charged $75.

The witness said he went to Ross Filippone and told him he needed a $75 cash advance on his Chargex card to take Lena out for a good time.

The witness said he subsequently signed a Chargex draft for $90 and received from Filippone a cash advance of $75, which the Crown has alleged represented a 20 per cent surcharge.

In a similar transaction with Joe Philliponi six days later, Ballantyne said, he signed a Chargex draft for $72.35 and received a cash advance of $60.

The trial continues today.

Sandy King rides as Lady Godiva, mid-1970s.

and his gang. In his report, Beattie noted that after wiretaps were installed on the Penthouse payphone, police intercepted a conversation between Eccles and a man named Wayne, who spoke about a delivery of drugs that Eccles was expecting. Beattie states that during the call, "Eccles told Wayne that he had people waiting on the street corners for them," and Wayne explained that he was too busy "capping up; it's still loose," and was not ready for delivery.

Lake's vice-squad investigation remained secret from other police working the area, such as Grant MacDonald. "Occasionally I'd see other guys from the department there in plainclothes, and we'd pretend not to know each other," MacDonald says. "I always thought it was weird until it came out much later that they had this investigation running."

Starting in early 1975, dancer Sandy King did two shows nightly at the Penthouse six nights a week, from Monday to Saturday. King had come from Isy's Supper Club to the Penthouse when she was just seventeen years old. She'd already been an experienced dancer after a run in Las Vegas, where she learned more than just the usual bump-and-grind routine. "I did a pretty good whip show," she laughs.

I could really smack myself and scream, but it was pretty classy! Thursday to Saturday was always packed and sometimes Monday was really busy too. The town was really jumping then; there were obviously less places to go. I usually got there around eight, as the shows would start at nine. When you got there that early, there would be just rows and rows of working girls, because the guys hadn't arrived yet. It was a pretty funny scene to walk in on.

We dancers weren't supposed to sit with the working girls. The guys [the Filippones]

Joe confers with exotic dancers in his office (behind Joe is Danielle Dean).

didn't want the customers to confuse us with them. But on some nights, Jack Diamond [the businessman, thoroughbred owner, and operator of Exhibition Park] would come in from the racetrack and bring a bunch of the dancers and working girls out for the day. The booze and the broads went hand-in-hand. You had a bunch of guys getting horny from the strippers, and there were working girls there to take care of them. In a way, both businesses fed off each other.

You could tell what mood Joe was in by the puffing of his cigar.

But King has nothing but fond memories of the club which elicit her quick laugh and vivid recollections of the nights she worked there. "One night I went upstairs to the steak restaurant and saw Mickey sort of having a food fight with Vincent Price [the actor]. They were trying to be sly about it, but were giggling while trying to eat, throwing a bun or some noodles here and there. It was kind of surreal seeing Vincent Price, of all people, and Mickey in a little food fight."

While she danced in the Penthouse's main Gold Room lounge, she also remembers John Eccles and Eddie Cheese and their crowd holding court upstairs; they often dated some of the dancers that worked downstairs. "They were tough guys you didn't want to mess with. But I also thought they protected that place. If somebody got out of hand there, those guys might take care of it and bring the guy out back for a pistol whipping!"

While Lake looked down on the Filippones, Sandy King has positive memories of how Joe, Ross, and Mickey treated both the working girls and the dancers. "They were great guys. With their cigars, you could smell them coming. You could tell what mood Joe was in by the puffing of his cigar. If he was puffing fast, he didn't want to be bothered. But if he was just standing

Cabaret 'kind of union shop' for hookers

By LARRY STILL

The prostitutes who allegedly plied their trade at the Penthouse cabaret considered the place "kind of a union shop," the Vancouver county court was told Friday.

Det. Kenneth Johnstone, a member of the city police vice squad, said he learned of the informal unionization when he posed at the club as an out-of-town businessman.

He said he expressed surprise when one of the women told him the price range for her services and asked her if it was the basic rate at the Seymour Street nightspot.

Johnstone said the woman replied: "Yes, we are kind of a union shop in here."

As an added convenience, he alleged, the woman said he could pay for her services by using his MasterCharge credit card to obtain a cash advance from the club's management.

Johnstone, a nondescript-looking man of medium height, looked every inch the small-town businessman out for some action in the big city when he took the witness stand.

He told Judge William Trainor he went to the Penthouse on Dec. 5, 1975, and in charged $70 for a short time of about 30 minutes or $100 for a longer period of about one hour.

When he told Candice he didn't have that kind of money on him, Johnstone alleged, she said he could get a cash advance on his MasterCharge card.

Johnstone alleged that Candice directed him to the manager's office where he met Ross Filippone, one of the six accused people in the trial.

The detective said he told Filippone: "I just met one of the girls, Candice. I propositioned her to take her to my hotel room and I don't have the $70."

He said he told Filippone the woman had advised him that he could get cash from the management on his MasterCharge card.

Johnstone alleged that Filippone replied: "What she didn't tell you is that there is a 20-per-cent surcharge."

The witness alleged that he asked Filippone to explain and he said he would have to sign for $90 to get a $75 advance, or sign for $84 to get a $70 advance.

Johnstone said he replied: "I guess I've got no choice in the matter. The banks are all closed at this time of night."

Jaques porduced to the witness a MasterCharge draft, dated Dec. 5, 1975, and made out for $84, which Johnstone identified as the one he had signed G. Burton.

After the alleged transaction with Filippone, Johnstone added, he walked back to his room at the Dufferin Hotel where he was joined minutes later by Candice.

Other police officers arrived at the room almost immediately, the detective said, and Candice was whisked away.

Johnstone was testifying against Joe Philliponi, Ross and Domenick Filippone, Jan Sedlak, Minerva Kelly and Rose Filippone.

They and Celebrity Enterprises, the Penthouse corporation, are charged with conspiring to live off the avails of prostitution and with conspiring to corrupt public morals.

During earlier testimony Friday, Det. Norman Elliot, who investigated the Penthouse for six months, said he considered Joe Philliponi and Ross and Domenick Filippone to be the club's principals.

Cross-examined by defence lawyer S. R. Chamberlain, Elliot agreed that he never asked any of the prostitutes if they paid money directly to the three principals.

Elliot also agreed that he never saw any of the three principals "exercise any physical control" over any of the women in the club.

Questioned further, he said he never saw club cashiers Minerva Kelly and Rose Filippone take any money other than the club entry fee from any of the women.

Elliot also agreed that he never overheard any conversation between Jan Sedlak, the club doorman, and Minerva Kelly whereby they discussed any arrangement to extract funds from the women over and above the entry fee.

During the cross-examination of Elliot, Judge Trainor suggested that Chamberlain was straying from accepted practice in his line of questioning.

"You should not stray from accepted, proper practice without getting permission from me," the judge said.

When Chamberlain said justice was being denied, Judge Trainor replied: "That really isn't up to you to decide."

The trail continues Monday.

---

there, puffing slowly, he'd usually want to be talked to. Some other club owners would look down on you. They thought that, just because you were a stripper, you had to be a slut. The Filippones were always fair. They treated you with respect. They had rules, too. They didn't want the hookers table-hopping or pestering customers. If they found out a prostitute had stolen something off a trick, they'd be banned."

King suggests that that very "rule" is what caused the hammer to drop in the winter of 1975. "That Christmas, there was a working girl who called herself Valerie Rose. She'd met a Japanese businessman, a well-connected guy, taken him back to his hotel, and got him into the shower. While he was in there, she stole his suitcase and took a cab right to her pimp's

Court told how woman tried to 'butter up men'

By LARRY STILL

The woman stood outside the Penthouse Cabaret on Seymour Street and proffered her bag of buttered goodies to the men who passed by.

To the unsuspecting, she appeared to be a particularly well-groomed popcorn vendor — but she didn't fool club president Joe Phillliponi.

He knew she was really a prostitute and she was buttering up potential clients.

Phillliponi told the Vancouver county court Tuesday that the popcorn was house rule against admitting unescorted women.

He told Judge William Trainor that the woman was a prostitute and she used the popcorn to lure men into escorting her into the club.

Philliponi was testifying at the trial, which today enters its fourth month, in which he and five other Penthouse associates face two morals charges.

He was cross-examined by prosecutor Roy Jaques on his earlier testimony that he tried in 1974 to keep prostitutes out of the club.

Jaques reminded the witness that he said he decreed, during one month in 1974, that unescorted women would not be allowed in.

Phillliponi said he tried to implement the rule, but it didn't work because the prostitutes devised a number of ploys to circumvent the rule.

"One woman stood outside the club with a bag of popcorn," he said. "She would offer a man some popcorn and then ask him to get her into the club."

He agreed with Jaques' suggestion that he had to abandon the rule because "the women were clamoring to get into the club" and were creating a nuisance on the sidewalk.

Philliponi said he next tried, but was forced to abandon, the rule that women who left the club with a man were not permitted to re-enter alone the same evening.

"We wanted to make sure the women were not going in and out just like a stampede ground," he told the judge.

When that rule failed because some women bribed the doorman to get back in, he continued, the club still tried to control the flow of prostitutes.

He agreed that some prostitutes continued to get back in, but said their presence in the club did not present a major problem for the management.

"The whole problem could have been eliminated if the police had pointed out the undesirables to us," he told the court.

Phillliponi said he was not aware that most of the women patrons in the club during 1975 were prostitutes, but said he was suspicious of some of them.

"I know from experience that in all bars and nightclubs these types of girls hang

said he would have "bounced them out on their ears" had he known.

He also denied the Crown's allegation that certain members of the Penthouse staff demanded tips from the prostitutes who allegedly frequented the club.

"Anyone, my brother, my niece, would have been fired had they done so," he said. "You don't spend thousands of dollars to bring in customers and then insult them by demanding tips."

Jaques referred Philliponi to a story that appeared Sept. 26, 1975, in The Vancouver Sun. It referred to police activity in the Penthouse and he suggested that it caused him to clean up the club.

Philliponi said the story's allegations that staff were demanding money from prostitutes caused him to fire cashier Minerva Kelly and doorman Jan Sedlak, both co-accused in the trial.

He said he had already warned his staff against demanding tips and The Sun's report was the story that "broke the camel's back."

(The story was based on a study, prepared by an official researcher from police files, which was presented to the B.C. Police Commission and released to the press.)

Jaques: "With the greatest respect to the press, (the story) could be a lot of baloney."

The prosecutor then proceeded to use the story as part of the Crown's case and put excerpts from it to Philliponi.

Philliponi said he thought the story was "exaggerated," but agreed that it did cause him some concern.

"It didn't mention the club by name, so there was no way we could sue," he told the court. "Otherwise, we would have taken action."

He said he had never found any fault with the way in which Kelly and Sedlak did their duties, but he fired them because he couldn't take any chances.

The prosecutor questioned Philliponi about certain men who sat in a group most nights in the club's dining room.

Jaques : "Did you suspect that some of your male patrons were pimps?"

Philliponi: "No, I did not."

He said some of the men who regularly sat in the club's dining room were suspected drug traffickers.

Questioned about the men's presence, he said he didn't bar them because police said they were under surveillance and told him to leave them alone.

Jaques reminded Philliponi of his earlier testimony that he once barred a black male from the club after a dancer had complained that the man had tried to get her to work for him.

Jaques: "Have you a particular dislike for black pimps?"

Philliponi : 'Some of my best friends are black — the Mills Brothers, for instance. I am not prejudiced. I dislike all pimps, black, white or yellow."

Jaques: "So in 1975, with the exception

---

place. They went through it and then drove to Stanley Park to dump the suitcase. They'd taken his wallet, but they'd also taken his passport, and that was serious. He went to the police. We all heard about it. The next thing you know, the cops hit the place."

After months of investigation that included twelve officers, photograph and wiretap surveillance, male officers posing as clients, and female officers posing as prostitutes, police entered the Penthouse on December 22 and arrested Joe, Ross, and Mickey on charges of "conspiracy to live off the avails of prostitution, corrupting public morals, and keeping a common bawdy house." In addition, doorman Jan Sedlak, cashier Minerva Kelly, and Mickey's daughter Rose were also charged because Lake believed they had profited from the tips they were given and cash they handled.

The family was stunned. Joe, Ross, Mickey, and the co-accused were termed "the Penthouse Six" in the newspapers, the club was padlocked by court sheriffs, its licence revoked, and the Filippone family banded together for its biggest fight yet.

Russ Chamberlain was a thirty-four-year-old Vancouver lawyer who'd only been practicing law for a few years when Joe and Ross Filippone came to his office to hire a lawyer in early 1976. "I'd never met them before. I'd certainly heard, when I was at UBC [the University of British Columbia] in the 1960s, that the Penthouse was the place to go if you wanted to find a prostitute and not get harassed for hiring them off the street. But I'd never even been in there before."

Chamberlain still remembers his first meeting with the Filippone brothers. "Joe was an amazing character. He was about five-foot-six and perhaps the same width! He had a good sense of humour, and was really a very astute businessman. Nothing fazed him; no problem was too big to solve. But I found Ross taciturn and quiet. He really struck me as the iron hand that ran the day-to-day operation of the Penthouse."

Chamberlain didn't know it, but he'd come highly recommended to the Filippones. "Much later, I found out that Les Peterson, the former attorney general of BC, and Angelo Branca, who by that time was on the Supreme Court of British Columbia, had recommended me to the Filippones. I'd appeared before Branca in court, but he and Peterson really only knew me by reputation. I gather they'd told the Filippones that if they needed somebody who would overturn tables to fight the case, I was their man."

The last notable trial of its kind in the old Provincial Courthouse before the Vancouver Art Gallery took over the building in the early 1980s, the case of *Her Majesty The Queen against Celebrity Enterprises Ltd.*, began in September 1976. Prosecuting the case for the Crown was Roy Jacques, pronounced "Jakes." Chamberlain was familiar with Jacques as a city prosecutor before the trial. Born in England, Jacques had the air of a man too prim to be exposed to the term "prostitute" or any of its more colloquial terms during the court proceedings, yet he prosecuted the case with relish. "His accent suggested he would have fit in well at the cricket grounds of Eton," Chamberlain

The next thing you know, the cops hit the place.

Constable Vern Campbell in the late 1960s, shortly before he transferred to the vice squad. Photo courtesy of Vern Campbell.

recalls. "Jacques was a prickly, sanctimonious guy with the moral righteousness of an English parson. He found the Penthouse and everything it stood for abhorrent. He was indignant all the time, with no sense of humour at all, so I constantly tried to make him the butt of every joke I could during the trial to get a rise out of him."

Presiding over the trial was Justice William Trainor. A balding, bespectacled man with sandy hair, Trainor's quizzical eyebrows framed his disapproving stare down from the bench to Chamberlain's courtroom antics. "Trainor and I were at constant war during the trial. He would sneer at me, and I had barely concealed dislike for him. There would be exchanges where he would address me, and I would say, 'I know your lordship is not speaking disparaging words of me but I would note for the record your lordship is sneering contemptuously at me.' This went on all the time!"

The events in Courtroom 214 of the Provincial Courthouse played out with the kind of lurid testimonies that packed the gallery and made for the kind of sensational headlines that the BC courts have rarely seen before or since. Witnesses for the prosecution ranged from a prostitute disguised in a wig and sunglasses who refused to identify her pimp (sitting in the same courtroom) for fear she would be beaten. On another day, a pair of fourteen-year-old schoolgirls told the court how they visited the Penthouse, hoping to turn a trick. Chamberlain aggressively cross-examined the prosecution witnesses, suggesting that they had been coached by the police or offered leniency on other charges if they testified against the Penthouse. He also argued that some Crown witnesses were prostitutes from the East End who had never even been to the Penthouse.

From the police department, Leslie McKellar took the stand, telling the court how the visiting Japanese navy "invaded" the Penthouse on shore leave in the summer of 1975. "There were so many Japanese customers coming in that some of the girls learned quite fluent Japanese," she said. In addition to McKellar, the prosecution offered testimony from two members of Inspector Lake's vice-squad team, Detectives George Barclay and Norm Elliot. Barclay was often on one of the pick-up teams, and Elliot had played the part of a crooked plainclothes cop trying to ingratiate himself into the Filippones' trust. Barclay and Elliot's testimony was meant to support the prosecution's assertion that the cover charges paid by the hookers and the cash advances on credit cards were part of the Filippones' conspiracy to profit from the prostitutes that frequented the nightclub. Chamberlain assiduously questioned Elliot on the stand about how many drinks he normally consumed in one night's surveillance at the Penthouse (Elliot admitted up to twelve), and suggested in court that he had even begun a relationship with one of the club's dancers, Miss Lovie. Elliot denied any relationship but admitted taking Miss Lovie to dinner.

Another Crown witness was a prostitute who stated she started working at the Penthouse one week after her seventeenth birthday and that, with her husband

24**** THE VANCOUVER SUN: THURS., SEPT. 30, 1976

Penthouse probe officer led champagne existence

By LARRY STILL

A policeman's lot is not necessarily an unhappy one — particularly if he is a member of the vice squad on an under-cover assignment.

Det. Norman Elliot has told the Penthouse trial he went to the Seymour Street nightspot almost every evening for five months, drank champagne and dined with a club dancer.

At the hearing Wednesday, Det. George Barclay said he went to the club on eight different occasions and was repeatedly propositioned by women, including those who knew his real identity.

He remembered in particular a woman named Emily Ribble, whom he found "easy to like," with whom he developed a friendly relationship.

Emily, the likeable hooker, apparently found George, the snappily-dressed vice squad detective, quite irresistible.

"Every time I see Emily, she offers me sex," Barclay told Judge William Trainor.

"She says, 'Come on, George,' and I say, 'I can't afford you, Emily,' and she says, 'It'll only cost you $30.'"

The $30 offer is a bargain. According to previous testimony, the rate usually quoted by women at the Penthouse ranges from $60 to $100.

Barclay agreed that he has known Emily Ribble for a long time and that she knows he is a member of the police vice squad.

Charged with conspiring to live off the avails of prostitution and with conspiring to corrupt public morals are Joe Philliponi, Ross, Domenick and Rose Filippone, Jan Sedlak and Minerva Kelly.

Barclay said he has investigated prostitutes' activities from the Bayshore Inn to the Stratford Hotel.

During cross-examination by defence lawyer Russ Chamberlain, Barclay agreed that he did "establish a working relationship" with some of the prostitutes around town.

He denied that he specifically told some of them that if they talked to him about others' activities they would not be charged with soliciting.

Chamberlain reminded Barclay that he told prosecutor Roy Jaques about an incident in which he gave a woman a quarter to feed the Penthouse juke box and she performed a strip tease dance to the music.

The defence lawyer informed Barclay that there is no coin-operated juke box in the Penthouse and there never has been.

Barclay: "Maybe I got ripped off for a quarter."

In continuing to test Barclay's credibility, Chamberlain got him to agree that a number of answers he gave at the preliminary hearing conflicted with his answers in the trial.

He agreed that, at the preliminary, he said Tony Pizani, an unindicted co-conspirator, was in the club on Sept. 11, 1975, and was acting as the M.C.

Informed that Pizani was no longer employed as the M.C. by that date, Barclay said he knew that was so and meant to say Pizani was in the club as a guest and took the stage in that capacity.

In another exchange, Barclay agreed that at the preliminary he swore that Sedlak was the club doorman on Nov. 7, 1975, but in the trial said the doorman was any one of three men.

"You approach your evidence that loosely that you are not concerned with the truth," Chamberlain remarked.

Questioned further, Barclay agreed that he had never seen Rose Filippone, the club cashier, collect any money from women patrons other than the $2.95 entrance fee.

He also said he saw Eleanor Harrigan, an unindicted co-conspirator, on one occasion receive $2 from a woman patron, but agreed that it was a tip to her as maitre d'.

Barclay also agreed that he never saw any of the other five defendants receive money from any of the women patrons in the club.

Jaques told Judge Trainor he expects to complete the case for the prosecution Friday. Chamberlain said he will be calling evidence for the defence and expects his case to take two weeks to complete.

The trial continues.

Examination by doctor shows prostitute wrong

By LARRY STILL

The judge in the Penthouse trial suggested Wednesday that a Crown witness may have perjured herself when she alleged she engaged in a sex act with one of the accused.

Judge William Trainor was commenting on a medical opinion which indicated that Ross Filippone was not the man who allegedly persuaded a prostitute to perform oral sex with him.

Filippone, at the Crown's suggestion, was examined privately by a urologist to determine if a certain part of his anatomy matched a description given by the prostitute.

He returned to the witness-stand Wednesday and advised the court that he had had a private consultation with the urologist.

Questioned by prosecutor Roy Jaques, Filippone agreed that the doctor "examined a particular part of the body and found no deviation from the norm whatsoever."

Jaques: "Did you commit a sex act of any kind with the prostitute?"

Filippone: "No, I did not."

Jaques: "I accept your answer without qualification or reservation whatsoever.

"In view of the medical evidence, the Crown is satisfied that the allegation concerning the act of fellatio is not true."

The prosecutor's remark caused Judge Trainor to ask if the Crown concedes that the prostitute was lying when she gave evidence.

Judge Trainor: "Are you telling me you accept that she committed perjury?"

Jaques replied that he was not alleging perjury, but was conceding that the prostitute was mistaken in her identification of Filippone.

Judge Trainor agreed that there is a conflict in "the nature of the particular part of the anatomy of this witness," but asked how it afected the rest of the prostitute's evidence.

Jaques said the prostitute made a "serious allegation" against Filippone when she testified Sept. 1 and the Crown now feels that the matter should be resolved.

"The Crown realizes that the (prostitute's evidence could not relate to this witness and he should not be under a cloud." Jaques told the judge.

Judge Trainor: "Is the Crown asking me to completely ignore the evidence of the prostitute? If you are, you are doing a good job."

Jaques repeated that he wanted to clear up the portion of evidence that related diretly to Filippone.

"Do you want me to ignore all of her evidence?"

Jaques: "No, I want you to ignore the portion that relates to the act of fellatio."

Judge Trainor: "All you can do is ask me to ignore all the evidence of the prostitute."

ni, Ross, Domenick and Rose Filippone, Jan Sedlak and Minerva Kelly.

At the opening of the Crown's case, the prostitute who made the allegations against Filippone also gave detailed testimony on her activities at the Penthouse.

She said she visited the club on numerous occasions and picked up clients whom she charged $60 to $75 for a 30-minute sex act.

The unnamed woman said she paid $2.95 when she first entered the club each evening and $2 to $3 for a table, but was required to pay a further $7 if she left with a client and wanted to return.

The Crown has alleged that members of the Penthouse staff demanded money from the 150 to 200 prostitutes who allegedly frequented the club each night.

Jaques has also introduced evidence that the management allowed male patrons, for a 20 per cent surcharge, to pay the prostitutes with cash advances obtained on credit cards.

During his evidence Wednesday, Filippone said all patrons, if they made a prior arrangement with the doorman, could leave the club for a short time and re-enter without paying again.

He denied the Jaques' suggestion that the prostitute didn't enjoy the privilege of free re-entry and had to pay again.

The witness denied the prosecutor's suggestion that a regular scene at the club was to see women leave the club with men and return alone.

"I can honestly swear that I never saw a lady leave the club with a man and return alone," Filippone said.

He said he asked doorman Jan Sedlak how many females returned in one night and Sedlak said never more than one or two.

Filippone agreed that it did occur to him that prostitutes went to the club to carry on their business, but said he was unable to keep them out as long as they did not commit an offence.

"I couldn't accuse anyone of being a prostitute," he added. "We got top legal advice on that."

When Jaques said Filippone could have hired staff to keep known prostitutes out, the witness said: "We have a police department to do that kind of work."

Jaques suggested that the club's doorman, cashier and maitre d' were all paid the minimum wage because the management knew they were demanding tips from prostitutes.

Filippone said the doorman was paid double the minimum wage.

Jaques: "You realized they would not work for that wage unless you allowed them to take their cut of the profits made from prostitutes re-entering the club."

Filippone: "That is absolutely false."

Jaques referred to a staff notice in which the management warned the staff against demanding tips from the patrons and suggested it was issued to "cover up

---

acting as her pimp, she had used the Penthouse as a headquarters, making $20,000 between February and July 1975. She also made a startling claim that she'd been required to pass an unusual test before being allowed to operate in the nightclub; she had to give Ross Filippone oral sex. Filippone fully denied her claim and Chamberlain insisted that his client take a lie detector test to prove his honesty. Later, when Chamberlain entered a physician's report to prove the woman was unfamiliar with his client's anatomy, the Crown considered much of her testimony useless. "If she did perform an oral sex act," Chamberlain told the court, "it was certainly not on Ross Filippone."[29]

The salacious testimony during the lengthy trial proved difficult for the Filippones' family life. "My kids got ribbed at school. It was embarrassing," Ross said. "It didn't help my marriage, either."[30] Ross's wife Penny agreed. "We had a lot of support from friends and family, but it was a tough time for the kids. Every night it was on TV and in the newspapers. I went every day to the trial in the beginning, but it was too much after awhile. I couldn't take it. Our marriage was rocky by this point, but I couldn't and wouldn't leave then. We really tried to rally around as family, but it certainly contributed to it getting worse." Ross and Penny eventually divorced in the mid-1980s.

The long shadow of John Eccles also appeared, albeit briefly, during the trial when Detective Elliot testified that the Penthouse upstairs lounge had become a meeting place for the heads of the "local mafia," a comment that even Joe didn't disagree with.

Elliot identified Eccles as the leader of the group. Chamberlain objected that all references to Eccles and his cohorts who, despite their criminal activities, were no more than patrons at the Penthouse, were simply not admissible as relevant evidence. Judge Trainor agreed. Although a significant portion of Lake's investigation focused on connecting Eccles to the Filippones, he had no evidence to prove it. While Eccles and his associates were well-known to the police, their names never circulated further in the trial and media coverage. The Filippone family consequently bore the brunt of the overall negative connotations in the minds of the general public, who believed that they alone were the "Vancouver mafia." The Filippones' Italian name seemed to support the rumours, at least in the minds of those who'd recently heard the titillating adventures of organized crime figures, from the real-life Joseph Valachi to the big-screen characters in the film *The Godfather,* released just four years earlier.[31]

Of the some 700 photographs of men and women coming and going from the nightclub taken by Inspector Lake's surveillance team in the unmarked police vehicle, only 200 were entered into evidence. The *Vancouver Sun* quoted an unnamed police detective as saying, "Let's just say a blackmailer could make a fortune. There were lots of distinguished gentlemen."

Chamberlain heard all the rumours. "There were apparently photographs of people low and high in the community—politicians, judges, and businessmen from every walk of life. But the police never disclosed

Let's just say a blackmailer could make a fortune.

(Left to right): Juror, court sheriff, Judge Trainor, Roy Jacques, and Russ Chamberlain (with arm outstretched). Photo: Brian Kent, *Vancouver Sun*.

the other photographs during the trial." Suspicious housewives reading the details of the trial in the newspapers were left to glance sideways at their husbands at the dinner table, imagining them on police negatives, remembering nights when they called home to say they were out "entertaining clients" and wouldn't be back until late.

Chamberlain defended the Filippones with considerable vigor and élan and captured his own share of media attention. *Vancouver Sun* columnist Alan Fotheringham regularly reported his courtroom antics, noting that "Chamberlain had the good looks of a second lead in a Hollywood western." He was known to hurl his eyeglasses onto the courtroom's oak table and spring to his feet with objections, as well as uttering "my learned friend" at Jacques in a tone that implied something less than respect.

Chamberlain's most dramatic move resulted when, in an effort to explain the complex layout of various rooms within the Penthouse building, he suggested to Justice Trainor that the court adjourn to the Penthouse itself. Trainor agreed with the motion. Thirty minutes later, escorted by two sheriff's deputies, the judge arrived with a court clerk and a stenographer and was met at the door by Chamberlain, Jacques, and the six accused. Newspaper photographers captured the scene at the Penthouse's front door, which ran in the next day's papers with the inevitable caption, "Here Comes the Judge."

This was the only time in British Columbia legal history that a portion of the proceedings took place in an exotic nightclub. Chamberlain acted as official tour guide, walking Justice Trainor and the entourage past the cashier's area and into the lower Gold Room lounge. With the court stenographer behind them furiously scribbling shorthand into the record, they passed a stairway sign in glittering letters that read "World of Girls" and were smiled down upon by large photos of near-nude exotic dancers like Gina Bon Bon and Suzanne Vegas.

Vancouver Sun reporter Larry Still, who covered the entire trial for the newspaper and was among the press entourage inside the bar, described this scene: "Trainor joined Ross Filippone behind the bar, so he could see how the drink of a rum and coke would be entered into the register and how credit cards were processed. About one hour into the tour, Chamberlain asked the judge for permission to smoke. Trainor assented and the smokers lit up with Penthouse matchbooks thoughtfully provided by the management. At one point, Trainor was left behind the bar alone to examine the bar by himself. While it was well past the noon hour, no one in the party dared to request a double from His Honour."[32]

"Joe and Ross welcomed the vigor with which I defended the case," Chamberlain says. "But I told them from the beginning, as soon as we drew Trainor as our judge, that we weren't going to win. Based on my assessment, I knew from the start he was going to rule against us. All we could do was set up as many grounds for appeal as possible."

Chamberlain was correct. On April 22, 1977, over

Saturday, October 9, 1976

After the facts in vice trial, Judge William Trainor, second from left, leaves Penthouse cabaret Friday.

Judge takes the stage for justice

Judge William Trainor walked into the Penthouse world of girls on Friday, stood on the cabaret stage and even went behind the bar, but it was all in the cause of justice.

He moved the Penthouse morals trial to the Seymour Street club for a first-hand view of the lounges, stages and connecting staircases.

Celebrity Enterprises Ltd. Joseph Philliponi, Ros Filippone, Domenick Filippone, Rose Filippone, Jan Sedlak and Minerva Kelly are charged with conspiring to live off the avails of prostitution and with conspiring to corrupt public morals.

Jacques, defence counsel Russell Chamberlain, the court clerk, the government court reporter, sheriff's officers and the accused — but no trial witnesses — went through the street entrance and climbed the carpeted stairs into the club's Gold Room.

They passed a stairway sign in glittering letters which read "world of girls", and were smiled upon by near-nude women in large photographs adorning the walls.

The visit was informal, with the judge, the lawyers and court clerk wearing street clothes and not the traditional court attire.

Judge Trainor stepped behind one of the several liquor-filled bars and watched while Ross Filippone rang up an imaginary drink (rum and mix) and showed

And gazing down at them from her picture above the bar was almost-nude dancer Miss Suzanne Vegas.

The judge later stood by as lawyers and others counted the chairs and tables in the lounges and noted their arrangement.

The Judge took note of the raised heavily-carpeted go-go pedestals in the cabaret, and stood on the lighted stage to examine the scene.

Judge Trainor and the court climbed more carpeted stair into a dining lounge, passed a sign saying the lounge featured topless dancing, and then visited a private VIP room with its plush decor.

He viewed another lounge where the pictures on the wall were of a bygone era of show business.

Crown calls the Penthouse 'a scandal in this community'

Door policy said to prove conspiracy to corrupt morals

By LARRY STILL

The Penthouse cabaret's alleged role as a marketplace for prostitution was described Thursday in Vancouver county court as a community scandal.

Prosecutor Roy Jaques contended that six associates of the Seymour Street nightspot formed a common design to obtain money from prostitutes by allowing them to ply their trade at the club.

"The goings on at the Penthouse, having regard to their scope and of the large number of people involved over a long period of time, was a scandal in this community," he said.

Jaques was making his closing argument at the trial in which four men and two women each face two conspiracy charges related to alleged immoral activities at the club.

Charged with conspiring to live off the avails of prostitution and with conspiring to corrupt public morals are Joe Phillipone, Ross, Domenick and Rose Filippone, Jan Sedlak and Minerva Kelly.

In his address to Judge William Trainor, Jaques argued that there was a concert between the accused by which mutual consent to the common design was exchanged.

He said the concert is proved by the club's door policy that required prostitutes, in contrast to other patrons, to buy a ticket each time they entered the premises on the same evening.

Jaques said the accused all benefitted financially from the door policy, which was carefully contrived and strictly enforced as far as prostitutes were concerned.

In addition, he added, the cashiers (Rose Filippone and Kelly) and the doorman (Sedlak) levied a charge whenever a prostitute bought a second and subsequent ticket on the same evening.

Jaques also reminded the judge of evidence that a prostitute, once inside the club, was not allowed to choose her own seat unless she paid a "gratuity" of $2 to $5 to the hostess.

"The efforts of the management and staff appeared to have been directed towards facilitating prostitutes to carry on their business of prostitution in an orderly and effective manner," he said.

Jaques said the women could not have survived the active disapproval of the management and, in fact, were encouraged to ply their trade on the premises.

He said the money the prostitutes paid to the club was part of their "operating costs" and was a necessary expense in using the premises to meet clients.

In exchange for the payments, he added, the club allowed the women to ply their trade without interference from the management, the staff or the police.

Jaques said the accused all benefitted financially from the door policy, which was carefully contrived and strictly enforced as far as prostitutes were concerned.

Even if the cashiers, the doorman and the hostess did not turn over their "gratuities" to the management, the Crown's case is still established, the prosecutor argued.

"It is contended that it is not possible that either Joseph (Phillipone), Ross or Domenick (Filippone) or any of the defendants did not know of this," Jaques said.

He argued that the very least that can be said is that the staff were allowed to "retain their ill-gotten gains as the price of their zeal and loyalty" in seeing that the prostitutes bought a ticket each time they entered the club.

Jaques said the evidence indicated that 50 to 165 prostitutes attended the club and the number averaged about 100 each evening in the period covered by the May to December, 1975, indictment.

He said the average door revenue from prostitutes alone each night, considering that some would leave and pay to return, would be at least $600.

Jaques also noted that the payments of $2 each to the cashier, doorman and hostess, considering multiple visits by the prostitutes, amounted to another $600 each night.

"Given that the alleged discriminatory practice against prostitutes was agreed to and carried out by all the defendants, the prosecution submits that the finding would lead to the conviction of all the defendants," he said.

"The dominant characteristic of the club was to participate in, and make profit from, the commercial activities of a particular group of persons —an assemblage of prostitutes actively plying their trade in the club."

Jaques reminded the judge that a primary requirement for a prostitute to ply her trade is accessibility to men but the initial contact with a client may bring her in conflict with the law.

He added: "The twin goals of advertisement and safety from police intervention may be difficult to achieve.

"It need hardly be said that the other risk that most prostitutes run is that of being at the mercy of the client who behaves violently and criminally towards her.

"It may be fair to conclude that the common prostitute works in an environment that is hostile to her. She is subjected to many forms of exploitation not known to her sisters."

The prosecutor reminded Judge Trainor that the law does not forbid a woman from "selling her body" for money but it does forbid any third person from bringing it about or profiting from it.

He said any group that arranges for prostitutes to be given facilities for meeting large numbers of potential clients, and profits from it, is liable to be indicted for a conspiracy to corrupt public morals, which is the second count on the indictment.

He said the arrangement "must tend to promote the activities of prostitutes, resulting in lewdness and fornication inimical to the well-being, health and happiness of the people of this country."

Earlier in the hearing Thursday, defence lawyer Russ Chamberlain concluded his closing legal argument.

He reminded the judge of evidence that the Penthouse spent $180,000 during 1975 to hire professional entertainers.

"If you are nothing more than a bordello, as the Crown would have this court believe, you don't spend $180,000 on entertainment," Chamberlain said.

In analysing the evidence against each of the accused, Chamberlain said:

There is evidence that Joe Phillipone knew there were prostitutes in the club but none that he profited from their presence. He attempted to control the entry of prostitutes into the club.

There is no evidence that Ross Filippone had an agreement with anyone to live off the avails of prostitution.

Domenick (Mickey) Filippone was not a director of the club, played a minor role and did not have an agreement with any other person.

There is evidence that Sedlak received gratuities but there is none that he gave any of his gratuities to anyone else.

There is no evidence whatsoever that Kelly participated in any scheme. She followed the policy of the club in charging all patrons a re-entry fee.

Rose Filippone gave her evidence "candidly and forthrightly" and said she never automatically deducted money from anyone.

Chamberlain contended that the Crown must prove an "over-all conspiracy" by the accused to obtain a conviction.

He agreed that the judge could find that there is no evidence against one of the accused but there is evidence of an over-all conspiracy by the remaining five.

The hearing continues.

---

fifteen months after they'd first been charged, Justice Trainor found Joe and Ross Filippone, Jan Sedlak, Minerva Kelly, and Rose Filippone guilty. Mickey was acquitted because he only acted as host within the club. Trainor fined them and sentenced Joe and Ross to sixty days in jail. Crown Prosecutor Jacques heralded the court's decision to close the "supermarket of hookers" that he had accused the Filippones of running.

The Filippones immediately filed for an appeal and posted a bond for the convicted, and a new trial moved to the British Columbia Court of Appeal. It was there that Chamberlain, along with lawyer Thomas Braidwood, who lead the appeal, argued the Filippones case to the higher court. Braidwood suggested that in order to live off the avails of prostitution, one had to be seen as participating in their profits. The lawyers asked: If a prostitute is buying a dress at the Hudson's Bay Company department store with the money she has made from her work, does that

By LARRY STILL

The morality play known as Regina versus Celebrity Enterprises provided good entertainment for jaded Vancouverites — but the long-running production represents an estimated $1.5 million bill for B.C. taxpayers.

And Joe Philliponi, one of the leading characters in the marathon drama, estimates that the bill facing him and his colleagues, including legal fees and losses from the two-year closure of his business, will total $600,000.

Now, with the Crown and the defendants faced with an estimated $2 million bill, the B.C. Court of Appeal, in effect, has decided that the entire production was an abortive exercise in criminal prosecution.

Another loser in the affair is the Vancouver vice squad, which fears that the appeal court decision will prompt unscrupulous nightclub owners to open premises specifically aimed at catering to prostitutes.

Sources close to the affair, in which the Penthouse Cabaret and five of its associates were charged with two morals offences, point out that the matter remained unresolved for 2½ years.

They estimate that the long police investigation, together with proceedings before three different courts, cost the Crown a total of $1.5 million.

The Penthouse affair began in July, 1975, when police began a six-month undercover operation at the Seymour Street nightspot and, in December, 1975, charged the club and its associates with conspiracy to commit the two offences.

After a six-week preliminary hearing in provincial court, the accused were committed on July 12, 1976, to stand trial in Vancouver county court before Judge William Trainor.

That trial, which opened on Sept. 1, 1976, and concluded on May 11, 1977, ran for 61 actual trial days, and involved 45 witnesses, as well as police officers, sheriff's deputies, lawyers and court clerks.

At the conclusion of the trial, Judge Trainor convicted Joe Philliponi, Ross Filippone, Jan Sedlak, Minerva Kelly and Rose Filippone of conspiring to live off the avails of prostitution.

He imposed fines totalling $235,000 and jailed the men for 60-day terms, to be served intermittently.

The county court judge acquitted all the accused on the second count of conspiring to produce a public mischief with intent thereby to corrupt public morals.

Second decision closes the book

The B.C. Court of Appeal today closed the book on the Penthouse morals case when it dismissed an appeal by the Crown.

In delivering a unanimous decision by the three-member court, Justice A.B. Robertson upheld the acquittal of the Penthouse Five on a second morals count.

The court agreed with county court Judge William Trainor that a charge of conspiring to produce a public mischief with intent to corrupt public morals is not an offence under Canadian law.

The five are: Joe Philliponi, Ross Filippone, Minerva Kelly, Rose Filippone and Jan Sedlak. Celebrity Enterprises Ltd., the Penthouse corporation, was also acquitted.

"Appeal" page A2

then make the store guilty? They further argued that the wording of the Crown's original charge was not specifically applicable to the Filippones. Justice A.B. Robertson overturned the convictions in December 1977.

The Filippone family celebrated their vindication. Despite the thousands of dollars in legal expenses and years of stress on the family, Joe and Ross felt redeemed. Inspector Lake and Roy Jacques, on the other hand, were crestfallen. *Vancouver Sun* columnist Denny Boyd claimed that Angelo Branca had later "seared the buttons of Inspector Vic Lake's uniform, charging the Vancouver Police Department officer with creating a Penthouse dossier that was a bundle of half-truths, quarter-truths, and untruths."[33] Lake's undercover operation and the subsequent legal proceedings were said to have cost taxpayers $2 million.

"The trial finished Jacques," says Chamberlain, who

From left: Ross Filippone, lawyers Russ Chamberlain, Tom Braidwood, and Rick Sugden, and Joe. Photo: *Vancouver Sun*, December 20, 1977.

went on to have a successful criminal and labour law practice. Ross later named his dog "Jakes" as tribute to the prosecutor who'd so relentlessly prosecuted the case and cast aspersions against him. "I at least got to yell his name at the dog and run him around the block as revenge," Ross laughed. "He was a great dog—a much better dog than who he was named after!"

Detective Norm Elliot returned to police work dejected, and Barclay, who had already transferred to the drug squad, was equally disappointed with the verdict of the case. Today Barclay is circumspect. "We were just guys trying to do the job we'd been ordered to do, but in hindsight, I don't know whether [it] was the right thing to do. When we closed the Penthouse, it really caused a lot of problems in the West End. The closure caused an increase in the number of prostitutes suddenly working on the street. What had been a situation kept indoors suddenly was a public nuisance." Critics of the police investigation later suggested that the closure of the Penthouse indirectly resulted in a climate in which sexual predators—such as Robert William Pickton, the convicted murderer of dozens of Vancouver sex workers—could flourish.

Al Abraham agrees. "It was civilized. The girls were safe there [in the Penthouse], and under cover. Big deal if the Filippones grabbed an end, but why shouldn't they? They paid the taxes and kept the place safe. If some weirdo like Pickton would have come in, Ross or those guys would have remembered him and known what cab number he and the girl had left in. They kept an eye out for people."

For police officers like Grant MacDonald who, in the aftermath of the Penthouse trial was promoted to the homicide division, the closure of the Penthouse upset the informal information network that they relied on, the tips from prostitutes about major criminals with whom they came into contact. "As far as I was concerned, the Penthouse was never a problem," says MacDonald. "I knew what was going on. But it was controlled there. After the trial, the hookers poured out into the streets all over the city, and it became like

If a prostitute is buying a dress at the Hudson's Bay Company with the money she has made from her work, does that make the store guilty?

The Vancouver Sun

Joe Philliponi cleared of bribery

Penthouse operator wins second appeal

LATE FLASHES

Joe in 1978 holding up a copy of the *Vancouver Sun* (from the September 20, 1983 edition).

trying to capture quicksilver to manage it again."

Retired Constable Bill Harkema, who worked the West End beat during the same shifts as MacDonald, agrees. "There were guys in the vice squad trying to write up as many vagrancy charges on prostitutes as they could. If a girl got charged enough under the Vagrancy C-Class citations, she'd have to go to court, and if your name was on those charge reports you'd get called in to appear. Some guys were making a killing in overtime with their court appearances. While guys like Grant and I were out there trying to do some good police work, catching real criminals, I just felt there were some police targeting the prostitutes so they could rack up their overtime. It was really frustrating."

Meanwhile, John Eccles and Eddie Cheese continued their criminal activities for years. Eccles would serve nine months in jail for heroin possession in 1977. In the 1980s, police suspected Eccles and Cheese of being involved in a drug rip-off that consequently resulted in the unsolved murder of a Kitsilano couple whose bodies were found naked, bound, and gagged in the bathtub of their home, which was set on fire.

"By the end of the '70s, drugs had overtaken Eccles and those guys," recalls Al Abraham. "The whole vibe was different, they went on to heavier things and I lost touch with that whole scene." Eccles dropped off the police radar by the late '80s, but on August 14, 2004, Royal Canadian Mounted Police were called to an accident scene in BC's Okanagan region. They discovered a mostly submerged Jeep in Deep Creek that had first been spotted by a passing motorist. Emergency crews used the Jaws of Life to extract the driver and lone occupant, but Kelowna RCMP stated that fifty-nine-year-old John Kenneth Eccles had likely been dead for twenty-four hours. The BC Coroners Service ruled that Eccles had been intoxicated at the time of the accident.

Despite Eccles' notoriety in Vancouver as a figure in the criminal underworld of the 1970s, Kelowna RCMP, unaware of his past, said that he had not been a person of interest to them and they had no evidence to suspect

By the end of the '70s ... the whole vibe was different.

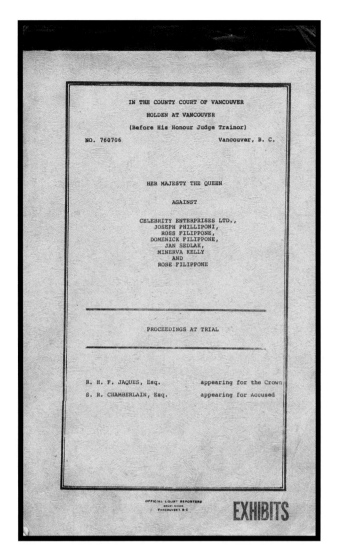

IN THE COUNTY COURT OF VANCOUVER

HOLDEN AT VANCOUVER

(Before His Honour Judge Trainor)

NO. 760706   Vancouver, B. C.

HER MAJESTY THE QUEEN

AGAINST

CELEBRITY ENTERPRISES LTD.,
JOSEPH PHILLIPONI,
ROSS FILIPPONE,
DOMENICK FILIPPONE,
JAN SEDLAK,
MINERVA KELLY
AND
ROSE FILIPPONE

PROCEEDINGS AT TRIAL

R. H. F. JAQUES, Esq.   appearing for the Crown
S. R. CHAMBERLAIN, Esq.   appearing for Accused

OFFICIAL COURT REPORTERS
COURT HOUSE
VANCOUVER, B.C.

EXHIBITS

his death was caused by foul play. In death, Eccles took the secrets and stories of his own nights at the Penthouse with him.

There was one remaining mystery from the trial. What had happened to the 700 photographs taken by the vice-squad surveillance teams? Rumours persisted that the photographs showed members of Vancouver's establishment coming and going from the Penthouse. It was said that these photographs would not be destroyed but kept permanently on file. In May 2012, over thirty-five years after hidden police camera shutters clicked away across Seymour Street, the author filed a Freedom of Information request to the VPD to access the photographs. While computerized records make accessing recent police records much easier, police archives prior to the late 1980s can only be referenced by antiquated paper index cards. The Vancouver Police Information and Privacy department found the index card regarding the case, but it didn't list a case reference number, which would have made it possible to locate the photos.[34] While the VPD admits that poor filing techniques and the absence of digitized records sometimes result in dead-end searches for old documents, one still can't help but wonder just who was captured in those photographs. And did someone, somewhere, discreetly urge a clerk to, if not shred them, then accidentally misfile them in the warehouse, making them difficult if not impossible to recover? For now, the photographs might as well be sitting at the bottom of Deep Creek with the ghost of John Eccles.

Despite the victory in the criminal case, Joe still had to fight another protracted legal battle with City Hall to renew the Penthouse liquor licence, which had been revoked during the criminal trial. He was forced to not only fight the province for the return of his liquor licence, but Vancouver city council as well for the return of his cabaret licence.[35]

When the Penthouse finally re-opened in September 1978, the glamorous days of well-heeled patrons mixing with the "rounders" were gone. The trial had stolen three years of the club's life, and the Penthouse found itself operating in a different world. The regulars had all gotten older or moved on, and although the Filippones had beaten the charges, rumours about the nightclub during the trial—both true and false—made what had once seemed mysterious and titillating now feel simply vulgar. "Maybe people thought they were going to be photographed or something," Sandy King suggests. "But when [the Penthouse] re-opened after the trial, it wasn't the same."

JoAnne Filippone agrees. "Something had been lost. Some of that special, higher appeal. When I first started working there, you would have never seen anybody come in wearing jeans and baseball caps. Society relaxed, and the dress code everybody had back then was gone. I don't know if that was a good thing."

The Penthouse was a long way from the nights when the city's smart set in their finery visited the nightclub. Now it was sparsely occupied by tourists and curiosity-seekers from the suburbs wearing T-shirts and running shoes who nursed one drink all night just

VII.
THE SHOW MUST GO ON

Joe and Ross, with Mickey in the background. *Vancouver Sun*, September 14, 1978.

Joe helping dancers dress, 1979. Photo: Brian Sprout.

to say they'd been there. But Joe soldiered on, hoping to show that the "hooker heaven" Penthouse days were gone. He even held "Family Days," when the public and employees brought their kids to the club so that all might see that 1019 Seymour Street wasn't the address for the local chapter of Sodom & Gomorrah.

"I used to have coffee with Joe once a week. I really liked him," recalls Mike McCardell. "He reminded me of some of the old colourful guys in New York I knew as a kid—a big Italian guy." McCardell, now a reporter for Global TV BC, was a crime beat reporter for the *Vancouver Sun* in the 1970s.

The exotic dancers had been given the day off, and Joe invited me and my family down. My wife was a little cautious. But my two kids, who were about eight or nine, were pretty excited because the place had such a reputation, and this was a place where kids didn't get to go!

There was a long lineup outside to get in. Joe came out and recognized me, took my kid's hands, and brought us in. As we walked past, people were holding their hands out to shake his hand or touch him. It was like people greeting the Godfather. Joe took us into the middle of the Penthouse main floor. He snapped two fat fingers and waiters brought a table out from nowhere, like something out of a movie. He put a towel over his arm and asked my kids what they wanted to eat. They ordered burgers and chocolate milkshakes.

Joe walked over to the kitchen and told this guy in his gruff voice, "I want two hamburgers and two chocolate milkshakes." The guy looks terrified. "We don't have milkshakes—this is the Penthouse! Joe tells him again, "I want two chocolate milkshakes." I didn't see it, but I figure the guy must have been terrified to tell Joe they couldn't do it, so he just ran around the neighbourhood looking to see where he could get two chocolate milkshakes in a hurry. A short time later, Joe returned—Joe Philliponi himself, the Godfather of the city—with a tray and two shakes and two hamburgers on it, with a towel over his arm, and served my kids. I'll never forget it.

Joe not only tried to re-invent the Penthouse, he also re-invented himself. He'd always been involved in charities, but in the 1970s became active with the Variety Show of Hearts telethon. "You could always count on Joe to show up every year with a $10,000 cheque," recalled booking agent Hugh Pickett, who had also been involved in the fundraiser.

Joe became active as a backroom figure and campaign donor in provincial politics. While the old allegations (and the nature of the business he ran) made it difficult for him to be directly acknowledged, on election nights, as winning candidates took the podium to make their acceptance speeches, the smiling

Joe, with Dee Dee Special, raises funds at the Variety Show of Hearts telethon, 1981.

face of Joe Philliponi with his white hair could often be seen applauding in the wings.

The family continued to have prestige in Vancouver's Italian community, where many considered them enterprising business owners who'd fought the city and won. "Joe was a leader and very enterprising," Ross recalled. "One time, Joe brought 200 Italians to a political rally. If Joe told 'em to stand up, they'd stand up. If he told 'em to sit down, they'd sit down. If he told them to clap, they'd clap. I always thought, *God forbid if he went to the toilet!*"

On an August evening in 1979, Mickey Filippone went to the Penthouse to start his evening shift. The club was just getting ready to open for the evening when Mickey asked his daughter Rose, who was working as a waitress, to order him a steak for dinner. He then excused himself to the bathroom. After some time passed, Rose became concerned and went to look for him, only to find that he had collapsed. His last works to her were, "I'm gonna be okay."

Mickey had been in two diabetic comas before, and despite warnings from doctors, hadn't changed his lifestyle. He fell into a third coma and would not live out the weekend. Domenic "Mickey" Filippone, the youngest of the four brothers, died on August 10, 1979.

The Filippone family was devastated, particularly Maria Rosa. Her vision had been failing for some time, but the distress of her youngest son's death was said to have driven her completely blind in mourning. It was the first death in the family since that of her husband Giuseppe, over twenty years earlier. With the bittersweet victory of the trial over and the business up and running again, it felt like one more terrible thing had befell them. Without Mickey, the family knew the future would be more difficult.

"He was a great guy, a great personality," recalls Al Abraham. "I don't think the Penthouse would have made it without him. He looked the part."

"Anybody who came down there, be it a lawyer or a dock worker, he made them all feel important. He was so good with people," recalls his daughter Rose. "He'd say to the staff that worked there, 'Take care of this guy. Give him the best seat in the house.' I think everybody thought he gave them the best seat!" Rose remembers

Mickey bowling in the 1953 A.B.C. Tournament in Chicago.

Mickey at the racetrack.

Mickey as a loving father whose sense of humour had helped keep the family's spirits up through the worst years.

One day I was heading out to the PNE [Pacific National Exhibition, an annual summer fair and amusement park in Vancouver] with my boyfriend at the time, and my dad asked me to go to the racetrack for him and place a bet on a horse. He loved the racetrack. He told me to bet on a single particular horse to win, place, and show, and he gave me—I'm not kidding—$500 for each bet. I really didn't know much about the races, but there I am, twenty-three years old with my candy floss and $1,500 in my purse to make these wagers for my dad. The horse came in first to win, So I threw away the tickets to place and show in the garbage, thinking they were no good.

I came home and Dad said, "Hey, we did good!" and I said, "Yeah, too bad you didn't get the other two." He looks at me confused and worried and says, "What do mean? Where are the other tickets?" I said, "The horse came in to win, not to place or show, so I threw those tickets into the trash."

Well, he almost had a heart attack! "Rose—you have to go back and find those tickets!" I didn't even know which garbage can I put them in, but I had to go back. They were just closing up and I pleaded with them to let me in. My boyfriend and I went through about four garbage cans while these guys were waiting to close up the racetrack. I was sweating and feeling terrible. Then—I couldn't believe it—I found the tickets. My dad never let me forget that one!

Sunday, September 18, 1983 began as a typically relaxed day for the Filippone family. With the club closed on Sundays, Joe did his usual routine of taking his mother to the farmers' markets in the semi-rural suburb of Richmond to get fresh vegetables and eggs for the week. Together they later visited Jimmy at his family home that evening, staying for dinner. "Joe was in a happy-go-lucky mood," Jimmy later recalled.

Joe returned home, sending a housekeeper away early, and had just said goodnight to his mother when Tony Pisani called. "Every Sunday, Joe used to come by to see me," says Pisani, who was then running an Italian gelato shop on Cambie Street. "He used to come and bring some of the dancers from the club or friends and get a cone for everybody. It was in the early evening and he hadn't come in. So I gave him a call at home to see if he was still coming in. He says, 'Yes, yes, Tony, I'm coming up soon, soon.' I happened to look at the clock in the store and it was 8:20 p.m., and we were closing at ten p.m., but he never showed up."

Joe was still at home, waiting for Sid Morrisroe. Joe had known Morrisroe since the 1940s. Morrisroe had fought at the Eagle Time Athletic Club in his youth. Now working in the plumbing business, separated from his wife and family, keeping company with an array of low-life gamblers at the race track, he remained an occasional Penthouse patron. Morrisroe had called Joe earlier that day about some plumbing work at the club that he wanted to reschedule for the evening. Joe had mentioned this to Ross and Jimmy.

VIII. BUONA NOTTE

Joe reclining in his office. *Vancouver Sun*, December 22, 1977.

Sid Morrisroe. File photo, *Vancouver Sun*, September 22, 1983.

Joe was relaxing in his armchair, watching television, when the doorbell rang. He got up and opened the door to find Scott Forsyth, a burly twenty-five-year-old journeyman painter from Smiths Falls, Ontario, who Morrisroe had met at the track. Joe knew Forsyth; he'd seen him drinking with Morrisroe at the Penthouse. Forsyth, with a bag of plumbing tools in hand, said that Morrisroe would be along shortly to do the plumbing work, and Joe invited him in. While they waited for Morrisroe, Forsyth then excused himself to the washroom, taking his bag of tools with him. The details of what happened next are taken from Forsyth's own testimony, as reported in newspapers at the time.

In the bathroom, Forsyth nervously removed a .22 calibre pistol from the bag, loaded it with one of the bullets he had in his pocket, and walked back into the living room.

"Okay, Joe, let's have the money," he said.

"There's no money here," Philliponi replied from his chair. "What the hell is this, some kind of joke?"

Forsyth moved closer and Joe realized he was looking down the barrel of a real gun. "Okay, okay, no problem," Joe said. He walked over to the safe in the living room, sank to one knee, and turned the dial on the combination lock while Forsyth stood watching him.

Forsyth glanced from the safe for a moment to Joe, and their eyes locked. Joe—neither nervous nor scared—looked directly up at Forsyth and said, "Don't kill me. Just go ahead," and motioned at the contents of the safe. "I won't even identify you in a line-up."[36]

Some people said that Joe Philliponi had felt lonely in the last few years; business was down, and the nightclub scene wasn't what it once was. His clientele was getting younger, but he wasn't. The dancers, bartenders, and waitresses that worked at the club had all been born after the Penthouse opened. When he talked with them, he didn't recognize their cultural references, and they didn't get his. Even the new hookers were a step down in class. In the old days they had been mature, well dressed, charming, and never violent. Now they were young, raggedy, and addicted to drugs. When he retold his favourite stories around the bar, he had to stop to explain to the younger staff who those once famous names were. None of them even knew who Les Brown and his Band of Renown were. After the trial, he'd once unwillingly booked some local rock bands; they were nice kids, but too loud for him. Joe was starting to feel his age. He joked about being an old man—but he was starting to feel a little more tired all the time. The nightclub life hadn't done wonders for his health, and he hadn't really taken care of himself. He'd had a prostate operation just a few years earlier, and was overweight.

Joe was the last of his kind. He'd lost many friends and business rivals over the years—Isy Walters from Isy's Supper Club, Ken Stauffer from the Cave, Bob Mitten from the Arctic Club—they were all gone. Even his friend Bill Kenny from the Ink Spots, who'd settled down in Vancouver, had died in 1978. And Joe felt the loss of his brother Mickey.

Okay, Joe, let's have the money.

Open safe in the Penthouse office, *Vancouver Sun*, September 20, 1983.

But he also had hopes for the future. There was no way he could stop now—there were too many family members who worked at the Penthouse and depended on him. What else was he going to do? They were sitting on too good a piece of property to pack it in now. Expo 86 was just a couple short years away, and Joe told friends he believed the Penthouse would be a hit with the tourists. He had a feeling that real burlesque was due for a comeback. He and Ross had been working on a show they hoped would bring back the old crowds, called "Casino de Paris," a full-blown costume revue they'd seen at the Dunes in Las Vegas.

Or maybe he thought of none of that—and what he did think didn't matter. Because when Joe Philliponi told Scott Forsyth that he wouldn't identify him in a line-up, Forsyth tensed, stared at him, and replied, "Oh, yeah? Fuck you," raised the gun, and shot Joe in the head.[37]

The murder of Joe Philliponi was just one of twenty-three homicides in the city in 1983, an average annual total for Vancouver at the time.[38] But it would be average in no other way; it was the most high-profile murder in the city that year and became one of the most notorious in Vancouver's history.

Jimmy found Joe's body the morning after the murder, when he began his maintenance duties for the day. When he opened the door, the TV was still blaring. Joe lay on the floor, next to the open safe. His pockets had been turned out, papers from the safe were strewn all over the floor, and cabinets and desk drawers were also opened. Jimmy immediately called emergency. Patrol Sergeant Brian McGuiness—later to become deputy Chief of Police in Vancouver—was first on the scene, followed by two ambulance paramedics. Jimmy also made a second call.

"Ross and I were in bed when the phone rang, and I picked it up," Penny recalled. "Somebody made some shocked noise on the phone, but it wasn't clear. I thought it was some crank call. About a minute later the phone rang again. It was Jimmy, who just said, 'Let me talk to Ross.'"

"I woke up to hear the strangest sound. I'd never heard it before," Danny Filippone recalls. "Like a wounded animal. It was my dad crying. I didn't understand what had happened. I got up and saw my dad getting dressed, and he told me that Uncle Joe had been shot." Danny got dressed himself, and drove his father down to the Penthouse. "It was a very sombre drive. We were just shocked and had no idea what had happened. I don't think we said anything the whole drive down."

They arrived to find a crowd of police, who had closed off Seymour Street. Ross and Jimmy discovered that their mother, who had been upstairs at the time of the murder, had slept through the incident. Jimmy had awoken her after finding Joe to see if she was all right, but did not tell her what had happened. She was too blind and hard of hearing to notice the scene outside where six police cars had already assembled.

Ross told police that when he'd last spoken to Joe, he'd said that he had to meet Sid Morrisroe that evening. Ross too had seen Morrisroe with Forsyth in

I didn't like his looks. I didn't like his style.

Penthouse club owner Joe Philliponi shot dead

The Sun

the Penthouse. "I didn't like his looks. I didn't like his style," Ross said of Forsyth.

With no signs of forced entry into the second-floor suite, police suspected that Joe knew his killer and had let in whoever his assailant was. Police asked Ross if he knew how much money and valuables the safe had contained. Rumours were that it regularly held a million dollars, and such rumours were part of the myth of the Penthouse. But the safe in the house wasn't the one that contained the lucrative weekend deposits from the bar, and never contained that much cash. Using the scattering of paperwork left behind, Ross did the math, which made the crime seem all the more grim. Whoever had killed his brother had done so in order to rob him of just $1,144.[39]

Friends and curiosity seekers descended onto Seymour Street, alerted by the morning media, as the city woke up to learn that Joe Philliponi had been shot and killed. "We were both dazed," Danny recalls. "I think [my dad] needed to get away from the madness for a bit, and we just slowly walked up Granville Street. We walked up a block or two and sat on a bench outside while the city was beginning its day and traffic drove by like it was any other morning."

Meanwhile, Sergeant Dennis Lannol told a press conference that Philliponi had been shot and killed. He did not say that police were already following up on Ross's lead and were looking for Morrisroe.

Once again the Penthouse was the lead story in the newspapers and on radio and television in the weeks that followed. On Vancouver's Commercial Drive,

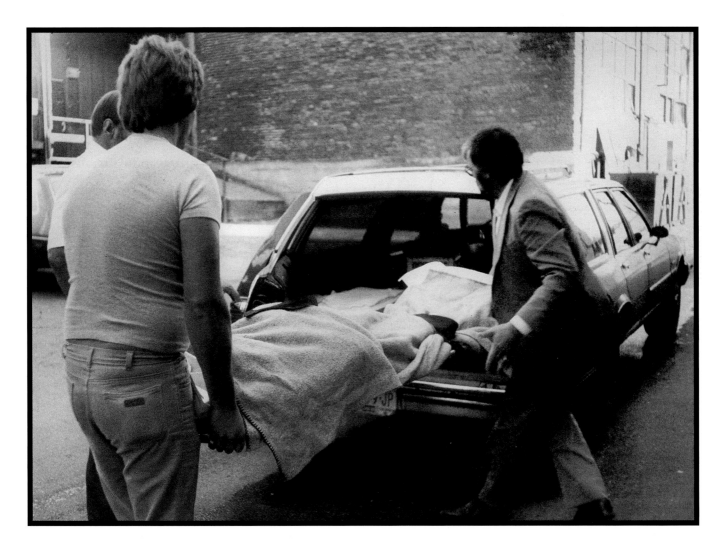

Coroner leading Joe's
body out of the Penthouse.
Vancouver Province,
September 19, 1983.

where Philliponi had been a familiar face on the street
that's traditionally been home to the city's Italian
community, there was an outpouring of shock over
his death. Antonio Luliano, owner of Café Italia (now
Caffe Roma), recalled how Philliponi helped him start
his business. "Everybody in the Italian community
loved Joe. He always wanted business to progress and
succeed. If somebody needed something—money,
help, whatever—he'd give it to them," Luliano said.[40]

The news also stunned old entertainment industry
friends like singer Frankie Laine. "I'm just shocked to

Everybody knew there were people that owed him money, and some of the people weren't good people.

hear about this," said Laine in a telephone interview from his home in San Diego at the time. "I remember Joe always as being a warm and generous person." In an interview from the Aladdin Hotel in Las Vegas, Sammy Davis Jr told reporters that "Vancouver has lost a part of its entertainment history." Davis said that he'd been a friend of Joe's for years, since he first performed at the Palomar. "Whenever I had a chance to go back to Vancouver, I used to hang out with Joe. To lose a friend like that is a real shock. A lot of people owe him a debt of gratitude, like the Mills Brothers, Billy Eckstine, and me."[41]

Vancouver Sun columnist Denny Boyd said that Joe "was never half as big as his wicked legend," and noted that, at his death, "he leaves more friends than enemies, which cannot be said of all men when they pass."[42]

"Joe was an amazing man. Nothing fazed him. No problem was too big for him. All he cared about was running that business. It was such a shock," Philliponi's former lawyer Russ Chamberlain recalled.

"I couldn't believe it," says dancer Sandy King. She'd seen Joe on her Saturday night shift at the Penthouse the day before the murder. "I was shocked—but in a way I wasn't. Everybody knew there were people that owed him money, and some of the people weren't good people. I first thought that, whoever had done it, they put a gun in his face and Joe probably told him, 'Screw you.' Joe didn't scare easily—all those guys [Joe, Ross, and Mickey] weren't afraid of anybody."

Joe's violent death added to his mystique as the "Godfather of Seymour Street." There was speculation about his connections with organized crime figures and some thought his murder was part of a mafia hit. Legendary bombastic alderman Harry Rankin was the most vocal, telling the *Westender* newspaper just four days after the killing, "I am sorry when any man dies before his time or has his life ended in such a brutal way. But let's not lose sight of the fact that the Penthouse was a hangout for whores, rounders, scroungers, crooks, and pimps. I don't think that Joe Philliponi was doing a service by keeping the prostitutes off the streets. I marvel that women's lib has nothing to say about the degrading, ugly performances staged at the Penthouse in the name of entertainment. I despise and I really object to glowing testimonials of that kind of person."[43] Rankin, however, was in the minority.

On the morning of September 22, more than 800 people attended the funeral for Joe at Vancouver's Holy Rosary Cathedral. In the same church where Filippone family weddings, christenings, and previous funerals had taken place, Joe's bronze coffin was carried up the steps by family members, including his nephews Danny and Joey. Vancouver has rarely seen a funeral attended by such a cross-section of the city. Stockbroker Basil Pantages, Whitecaps soccer team chairman Herb Capozzi, and retired Supreme Court Judge Angelo Branca sat beside musicians, club personalities, hookers, and dancers wearing tight black slit skirts, rounders with diamond rings on their pinky

Front page of the *Vancouver Sun*, September 22, 1983.

I thought to myself, *I'm going to get this guy.* We all knew he had something to do with it.

fingers, and strangers who'd simply come to pay their respects. It was just as Joe would have wanted it—a full house.

There was one significant woman not in attendance at the funeral—Joe's mother. Maria Rosa, now ninety-two years old, blind and almost deaf, had been in such frail condition that the family decided to postpone telling her about Joe's death. They discussed having a doctor on hand when they did, and slowly prepared her for the shock.

Joe was buried at Ocean View Cemetery near his youngest brother Mickey in a graveside ceremony attended by 200 close friends and family members. When Rose Filippone visited her father's grave, she often left a cigar at his graveside.

Police questioned Sid Morrisroe just hours after the killing. He'd maintained his innocence from the beginning, stating he'd cancelled the meeting on the night of the shooting and provided an alibi, having been seen at a bar that night. As he became a known suspect, Morrisroe told police and the media that there had been a $300,000 "hit" placed on him by the Filippone family. Ross denied it, and police found no evidence of it. But he had no idea how close he'd come to street retribution. Days after the funeral, twenty-year-old Danny was working at his job as a ticket seller at Exhibition Park (now Hastings Racetrack) when he recognized Sid Morrisroe walking through the concourse. "I couldn't believe it. We were all still so upset. I thought to myself, *I'm going to get this guy.* We all knew he had something to do with it.

"He was standing there facing the racetrack. I left my window and ... started walking up to him, clenching my fists. I got about twenty feet behind him, and suddenly two undercover detectives jumped out of nowhere and grabbed me by the shoulders, hustled me away, and calmed me down. Morrisroe was already under surveillance. I don't think Sid ever even saw what happened or how close it came."

The snare of the police tightened, and on October 3, an investigation led by Detective Joe Orth led to the arrest of Scott Ogilvie Forsyth, who'd drunkenly bragged of the killing to a waitress he was trying to impress. While Forsyth was in custody, he revealed further details of the murder to his cellmate, an undercover RCMP officer posing as a heroin dealer. After Forsyth realized he'd unwittingly made incriminating statements, he confessed the details of the whole plot. Forsyth cooperated with police to intercept and record a telephone call he made from the Vancouver Remand Centre to Morrisroe, where they discussed the robbery. After weeks of surveillance and repeated interviews with Morrisroe, police finally arrested and charged him. After his arrest, Constable Bill Harkema drove Morrisroe to jail in a patrol car. Harkema took a detour down Seymour Street, and drove by the Penthouse. "Morrisroe saw where we were driving. When we passed by, I wanted to see how he'd react, if he'd say anything. Sid slumped in the back seat and muttered, 'What did you do that for?' like he was insulted he'd been caught, and he knew he was going down."

... like he was insulted he'd been caught, and he knew he was going down.

What played out during the murder trial and over the following years would be enough to fill a book of its own. Forsyth testified that the plan to rob Philliponi was Morrisroe's from the beginning. Morrisroe owed Philliponi $6,000 and told Forsyth about the storied amount of cash sitting in the Penthouse safe. Morrisroe supplied the gun, but backed out of going to Joe's apartment that night. It could be said that the nightmare of the 1976 trial was playing out its final card. There had been so much conjecture about how much money the Penthouse was making and what was stashed in that safe that the rumours fanned the flames of Morrisroe's and Forsyth's greed.

Forsyth testified that, on the night of the shooting, he'd panicked and shot Philliponi after he said he'd never pick him out of a line-up. Morrisroe had suggested that Joe was connected to the Vancouver underworld and Forsyth suddenly feared that he wouldn't even make it to a police line-up before Philliponi had him killed.

Morrisroe later claimed that police had overlooked evidence when they first arrived at the murder scene, and that they failed to interview the housekeeper Philliponi sent home the night of the shooting. None of it convinced a jury. Both men were convicted of first-degree murder on June 13, 1984, and given life sentences of twenty-five years.

The story took a further twist in 1993. Morrisroe's daughter Tami was visiting her father, imprisoned at the minimum-security Ferndale Institution near Mission, BC, when inmate Salvatore Ciancio noticed her, and he liked what he saw. Ciancio fabricated a story that he was a distant cousin to the Filippones and that he knew that her father had been framed for the murder. He told her that Ross Filippone contracted the killing.

Tami, who was eager for any information to clear her father, fell for Ciancio's story. When he was released from jail, Tami struck up a relationship with him, hoping to learn further details to free her father. She essentially went undercover, taping her conversations with him. Ciancio always held back, changing the subject if she pressed him. Although she was already married, Tami married Ciancio to gain his confidence. Ciancio told Tami, who entered the witness protection program in 1996, that he belonged to a drug ring connected to a series of grisly underworld executions in 1995. Despite years of investigation by the RCMP, Ciancio was later acquitted in two trials that resulted in hung juries.

Sid Morrisroe served nineteen years of his sentence before he was granted early parole in 2002. He'd been a model prisoner but was in ill health in his remaining years. He died peacefully in a care facility in 2010, and Tami said she was grateful for the few short years out of jail she was able to spend with her father.

"The only regret I have is not proving his innocence," Tami told the *Vancouver Sun* when her father died. "It's the one thing I wanted to do—to clear his name."[44] That Tami put herself in so much personal danger to prove her father's innocence, that she accepted without question Ciancio's allegation, and that her crusade was essentially instigated by Ciancio's "pick-up line,"

Sid Morrisroe. *Vancouver Province*, March 16, 2000.

Maria Rosa and Giuseppe Filippone, c. 1940s.

remains astonishing to the Filippone family, who deny any family relationship, distant or otherwise, to Ciancio.

Ross Filippone told the author in 2007, "It's in the past now. I went through enough with the legal matters and victim's impact [statements]. I don't want to see or hear about Morrisroe. I think he should have served another five. I know he's maintained his innocence. What else is he gonna say?"

Scott Forsyth spent the next twenty years in prison for first-degree murder. At a parole hearing, he discussed the crime in detail, expressing remorse, admitting he was heavily intoxicated at the time of the murder. During his sentence, he participated in a number of alcohol and drug programs, and violent "offender relapse" prevention courses. Forsyth was granted full parole in 2004. In 2012, almost thirty years after the murder of Joe Philliponi, he declined to be interviewed for this book.

The year 1983 saw the passing of another Filippone. On Christmas Day, less than four months after Joe was killed, Maria Rosa Filippone died at age ninety-two. The family had never told her about Joe's death, "but I think she knew something was wrong with Joe," said Ross. Weeks before her death, she'd fractured a hip and had been in hospital recuperating. She was blind and almost deaf, and didn't seem to want to improve, refusing at times to eat or drink, sometimes pulling the intravenous needles from her arms. Ross went to visit her to wish her a Merry Christmas, and while he was there, she died quietly.

"With Joe's death, the energy left the family," said

Penny Marks. "Neither Ross, Jimmy, nor their sister Florence, who worked as the club's bookkeeper, had the strength to step into Joe's shoes. We all wondered what was going to happen with the business."

Ross seemed like a logical choice to take over, but he was less willing to fulfill the demands of working long hours at the club. He'd given up drinking and smoking and changed his lifestyle; he became a health enthusiast and racquetball player in seniors' matches and tournaments around the world. "It's completely the opposite of my old days, when I went to work at seven and came home at five!" he said. It was obvious the Penthouse would need someone new to lead it into the future.

Ross Filippone and his mother Maria Rosa.

The night Ross's son Danny was born in 1963, legendary comedian George Burns—in attendance as a guest at the Penthouse that night—personally handed out celebratory cigars to the nightclub patrons.

Visiting celebrities were a regular part of Danny's childhood. "I remember my father bringing home Duke Ellington, [hockey player] Stan Mikita, Tony Bennett, and others for dinner. They would have these big parties, where Dad hosted casino nights for friends and rented gaming tables. I remember one night when I was a kid, I wanted to go to bed, but there was a roulette wheel in my bedroom, and I couldn't. It was just part of the scenery when I was growing up."

Exactly what his father's occupation was remained somewhat of a mystery to Danny as a child. The nightclub was something his father did after Danny's bedtime, but there were certainly moments that suggested Ross was different from his friends' fathers and uncles.

In 1974, as a tip of the hat to the early 1970s fad of naked "streakers" running through public places, the Filippones decided to pull a prank of their own. "My uncle took me to a Vancouver Canucks game at the Pacific Coliseum with these three girls in full-length mink coats," Danny recalls.

IX. CHANGING OF THE GUARD

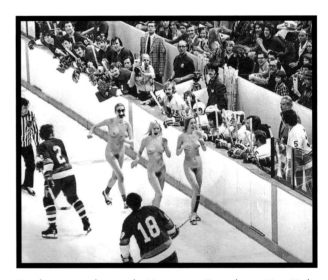

Penthouse streakers at the Vancouver Canucks vs. New York Islanders hockey game, Pacific Coliseum, February 2, 1974.

I didn't know them; I just thought they were friends of my dad. We had great seats, right down near the ice. I was eleven years old and just excited about the game. I had no idea that Uncle Joe had paid off somebody at the Coliseum to leave the arena gate to the ice unlocked. Sometime in the second period, during a stop in play, the girls put skates on, threw off the mink coats, and streaked across the ice past both benches and out the other side to a Diamond cab waiting to take them back to the Penthouse! Everybody

was howling and cheering, and I was just so red-faced shy, I couldn't believe it. But I still hear about the incident on sports-talk shows; it's in the fans' top-ten lists as one of the all-time favourite moments in the Canucks' history.

... and I think I cried while walking back to the bar, I was so confused!

The Filippone name was well-known when Danny was growing up. "There weren't many other prominent Italian families in Vancouver. There were the Capozzis for wines, the Lenarduzzis for soccer, and the Filippones had the nightclubs," he says. During the 1970s court trial, all of the family experienced some of the occasional discomforts of bearing the Filippone name, even members of the younger generation like Danny. "It was a confusing time. None of the kids at school asked me about it. Maybe they were afraid to ask. My parents sheltered us from a lot of that, keeping us busy, but it was a dark time."

Ross took on the role of head of the family after Joe's death, but he knew the Penthouse would need somebody with the right energy and enthusiasm to take it into its next chapter. While it's easy to assume today that Danny's destiny was to run the Penthouse, it was not always that certain. In his early twenties, he hadn't thought seriously (any more than most people of his age) about his long-term career plans. "I was basically into playing sports and meeting girls!" he says. When he began working as the club's only male waiter one night a week, he "didn't know a damn thing. My first order," he remembers, "this guy asks me for a 'Fifty-Seven Chevy with Massachusetts tags on it—neat,' and I think I cried while walking back to the bar, I was so confused!"

Danny vividly remembers being called to meet his father in their home, just three months after Joe's death. "Dad said, 'You have to make a decision. We have to know, as a family, if you want to do this full-time.' It was a lot to absorb at once. They wanted to know what direction things were going in and if I'd take over the reins. I said I'd do it. My heart was in it, and I liked it."

Joe's legend still cast a long shadow at the Penthouse. "It was weird the first couple of years after he was gone. I could still see him around and hear his voice. I have lots of great memories of Uncle Joe." But after at first co-managing with his father, Danny learned quickly, and he brought his own ideas to the club. He would choose a new dancers' talent agency and, while respecting the history of the room, began some much-needed renovations.

The Penthouse experienced a growth in popularity due to Expo 86, and a number of new Vancouver strip bars opened in its wake, including Champagne Charlie's, the Austin Flash One, and the Niagara, as almost every hotel bar put in a stage and booked exotic dancers. Danny would see the fads come and go. Within a few years, the thousands of exotic dancers working in Vancouver would dwindle from 4,000 to probably less than 200, and much of the Penthouse's competition again disappeared. "We're back to where we started in many ways," he says. The Penthouse is now, in 2012, one of the city's only remaining exotic show lounges.

And though the exotic dancers are still a feature, the club under Danny's management has opened up

Joe at the office.

Musician Steven Van Zandt with Danny Filippone, 2004.

Danny and R.E.M.'s Michael Stipe, 2007.

the venue for private functions, sports nights, and gay and lesbian parties. The club hosts performances for the Vancouver International Jazz Festival and concerts by alternative local musicians from Bif Naked, Dan Mangan, Maria in the Shower, and Rio Bent, to one local band whose name might have raised the eyebrows of some of the old clientele—Pepper Sprayed by Hookers.

Danny soon unveiled a wall of photos of new famous visitors to the Penthouse and needs little prompting to tell anecdotes about them with the characteristic ebullience and unique Filippone rhythm and tenor in his voice, the same way his father and uncles told stories of the stars in their day.

When Marilyn Manson stopped in at the Penthouse a few years ago, for example, Danny says, "He never paid his bill,"[45] and when Bruce Springsteen's sidekick Steven Van Zandt came to town, he called Danny to ask if, before the club opened for the night, he could just stand on the club's historic stage.

Danny has enjoyed operating the Penthouse without any of the notorious police-investigation issues that his father and uncles faced, but has kept the sense of fun and mischief that occasionally results in attention from the authorities. In 1997, when US President Bill Clinton visited Vancouver as part of the APEC meeting, during the height of the Monica Lewinsky scandal (Lewinsky was the White House intern whose relationship with Clinton jeopardized his presidency), the Penthouse marquee read, "Welcome President Clinton: Our Lips are Sealed."

"A few days before the summit, I got a call from somebody at the White House who was in charge of planning Clinton's motorcade route," Danny says. "Driving down Seymour Street, past the Penthouse, was one possibility, and they asked me to change the marquee. It had already been up for a few days, and I wasn't in the mood for a personal visit from the US Secret Service, so we changed it!"

Local history tour groups now visit the Penthouse to hear about its place in entertainment history, old tales about the liquor raids, and anecdotes of famous actors and musicians. They see vintage upstairs lounges now closed to the public and mostly used for film shoots for everything from *Star 80* (the 1983 Bob Fosse film about murdered *Playboy* playmate Dorothy Stratten, who was from Vancouver), Avril Lavigne and Snoop Dogg music videos, and the 2005–2007 CBC TV drama *Intelligence*, where it played the fictional strip-club the Chick-a-Dee.

Ross Filippone lived to see how local heritage groups would come to take an interest in the Penthouse, and although he handed the business over to Danny, he kept an eye on the nightclub. "I still enjoy coming down to the Penthouse once a week, just to check out the nightlife," he said. Ross passed in October 2007, aged eighty-four.

Jimmy Filippone passed away in February 2008. Perhaps the least well-known of the brothers, he was outwardly the most reserved, and some assumed that his early boxing days had left him a little slow of wits. But his shy nature hid a sharp sense of humour that was better known to his close friends and family.

Danny with Nickelback's Chad Kroeger, 2005.

Impresario Bruce Allen and Danny, 2007.

The Penthouse plays a strip club in the film *Star 80* (1983) starring Eric Roberts.

Ross at the Penthouse, c. 2005.

Jimmy, c. 1950s.

Left to run Diamond Cabs, Jimmy never had the high profile of his brothers. After the cab business was sold and amalgamated with Black Top Cabs, Jimmy became the Penthouse's building manager and maintenance man. "He loved to tinker," says his daughter JoAnne. "He often arrived to begin his work day while the other three brothers were leaving, after being there all night."[46]

When lawyer Russ Chamberlain drives by the club today, he thinks of his nights there in the late '70s, after they won the case. "I think the Penthouse should be remembered as a place where all walks of

After the fire, 2012.

life went, met, and had a good time. The Filippones have done nothing but benefit the community with their contributions to business and social sense. It's provided a lot of great entertainment over the years for a lot of people—and a lot of laughs."

The legacy his father and uncles entrusted to Danny almost completely disappeared in the fire of November 2011. By then, more than twenty-five years had passed since he'd driven his father to the Penthouse on the terrible morning of Joe's murder. This time he made the drive alone. "It seemed like I was the only one on the road. As I came over the Second Narrows Bridge, all I could see was smoke billowing from where I knew the Penthouse stands. The news was already on the radio, and my phone was ringing non-stop."

Filippone pulled up two blocks away from the club—as close as he could get because emergency crews blocked the street—left his engine running, and raced down the sidewalk, bursting past the yellow tape that cordoned off the area, only to watch helplessly from the alleyway as fire crews broke in doors and showered the rear of the building with water from their hoses. Within a couple hours, Danny learned that, despite serious damage, the fire had been contained to the back of the building. None of the photos in the Penthouse's extensive archive—many of the very photos in this book—had been destroyed. "It was an amazing relief, and I finally had a chance to breathe. I had 165 text messages in two hours from people all across Canada, asking what had happened, and if everybody else was okay."

While Danny optimistically told the media he'd re-open in two weeks, building restoration crews revealed asbestos in the building. Significant renovation had to be done, and Danny took the opportunity to fully renovate the main bar. After five months, Danny officially announced that the Penthouse was re-opening. "There were times when the renovation looked so complex and costly, I had to question whether it was worth it. But the media interest in our re-opening was unbelievable. It was at that point that I knew that people did care. Vancouver cared."

With a roving searchlight beaming into the sky, on Thursday April 5, 2012, the club re-opened to a packed house of friends, family, old patrons and staff, retired police, media, local musicians, fellow club owners, and well wishers, who all watched Danny, with the aid of legendary local radio DJ and Rock and Roll Hall of Fame inductee Red Robinson, cut the red ribbon.

One of the longest-running family businesses in Vancouver, the Penthouse has endured liquor raids, police investigations, bureaucratic hassles, and the murder of a family member. It would be easy to sympathize with any business owner who decided to pack up and leave after facing such hurdles. Vancouver would do well to recognize the Penthouse today. That the Filippones didn't pull up stakes is perhaps testament to the family's loyalty to the city.

Thanks to the real-estate boom in Vancouver in the last thirty years, the club's location makes the property worth a fortune. Danny regularly receives offers from

The Penthouse's grand re-opening after the fire, April 5, 2012. Photo: Rebecca Blissett.

Danny Filippone, 2012. Photo: Rebecca Blissett.

Promotional materials for the Palomar (top) and the Cave (bottom) nightclubs.

prospective buyers for the land. He looks at all of them, but he's consistently declined each one, noting the club's history and its family connection. "The Penthouse will always have its past, and that's what makes it different [from other clubs]," he says. Even the family home next door is historic. The house that Maria Rosa and Giuseppe Filippone had purchased in 1932 is now the oldest residential house in downtown Vancouver, according to Vancouver house historian James Johnstone.

That building too is still revealing its secrets. After Joe's and Maria Rosa's deaths in 1983, the house remained vacant for some years, frozen in time like an homage to 1970s décor. In 2004 one of Danny's bar managers, Gwyn Roberts, moved in. "Nothing had been touched since Maria Rosa passed," Roberts says. "There were stacks and stacks of bed linens. I figured I'd donate them to the Salvation Army, so I started packing them in boxes. As I was putting linens in a box, I felt a lump in one of the bed sheets and found a few hundred dollars had been sewn into the sheet!" Scott Forsyth might have looked in the linen closet rather than in Joe's safe on that fateful night in 1983.

When Roberts moved in, he also found Joe's old suits, still hanging in the closets where Joe'd left them. Joe's striped and checkered jackets, suits, and ties were trademarks of his public image. Roberts packed up Joe's entire wardrobe—being careful to look through the pockets for anything Joe might have left behind—and donated the clothing to the costume department at the Vancouver Playhouse, where theatre-going audiences would unknowingly appreciate the legacy of Joe Philliponi in colourfully dressed stage characters for years (although, sadly, the Playhouse closed down in 2012).

So many of Vancouver's storied cabarets and clubs of yesteryear—the Palomar, the Cave, Isy's, the Quadra Club, the Pender Ballroom—are long gone. Even more recent venues such as the Smilin' Buddha, Cruel Elephant, Town Pump, and Richard's on Richards are no more—having been torn down for condo developments, left neglected, gutted, or redesigned as template nightclubs with little real character or warmth. But friends from the nightclub's golden age still come back to visit. In the 1980s, Frank Sinatra called on Ross at the club. In March 2008, producer Quincy Jones was speaking in Vancouver when he told an audience of his fondness for the city, which he'd first visited touring with Lionel Hampton in the early 1950s. He thanked the Filippone family and the Penthouse nightclub for the warm welcome they received, not just as black entertainers in an unfamiliar town, but as friends.[47]

The Penthouse has been recognized by the BC Entertainment Hall of Fame as an Historic Venue. The only other two venues recognized by the Hall are the venerable Commodore Ballroom and Orpheum Theatre, still standing as entertainment institutions for multiple generations of Vancouverites. The entertainment business has changed, however; many larger touring shows today appear at show lounges or casino theatres far from the downtown Vancouver

Ross, musician Dal Richards, and impresario Drew Burns at the BC Entertainment Hall of Fame Historic Venues ceremony, Commodore Ballroom.

Dal Richards (left) with Joe (centre), Don Mills of the Mills Brothers (second from right), and Dal Richards Band singer Beryl Boden (right), 1948.

core. But one wonders if, in sixty years, Vancouverites or visiting entertainers will nostalgically recall their evenings at those venues. Will places with the character and history of the Penthouse even exist?

Ross with friends under the original Penthouse marquee, 1957.

On a warm summer Saturday night, the Penthouse is busy. People play pool, stand at the bar, or sit at tables in the lounge to watch the dancers. It's doubtful that either the dancers or the young men and couples watching them know exactly who Frankie Laine or Jimmy Durante are—or most of the other old stars, for that matter, though they continue to smile down on the patrons from photographs on the club's walls.

Much has changed since Joe and his brothers opened the Penthouse in the 1940s. The clothing—and lack thereof on stage, for a start. The urgent bass beat that Sassy Scarlett dances to is a long way from Nat King Cole's "Stardust." But the sound of laughter and glasses clinking around the bar is the same. You can see far more on the Internet, without ever leaving your home, than you can in an exotic-dancing bar. But people still like to get together in person and take in the nightlife, have a drink, relax, flirt with a dancer, and have a good time.

As increasing numbers of condominium towers now stare down at the club, it seems ironic for a building so small (when compared to its neighbours) to call itself the Penthouse. But Danny Filippone can stand outside the nightclub's front door, just as his father did before him, watching traffic drive by, and see the building's iconic green-and-pink neon glowing over Seymour Street. "We're staying put," he says. "Business is good, so why would we want to stop now?" Considering that the landmark that holds so much history—his family's and the city's—is still standing, he's got a right to be pleased.

X. SEYMOUR STREET SERENADE

The club has withstood everything from vice-squad inspectors who worked tirelessly to see it shut down, the murder of the man who was so much a part of the nightclub that his death nearly spelled its demise, the fads of its competitors, a major fire and, so far, the threat of the wrecking ball. The Penthouse still has a few cards to play, and if Danny Filippone has any say, last call won't come to Seymour Street anytime soon.

Two different views of Seymour Street from the front of the Penthouse, 1970s.

ACKNOWLEDGMENTS

Asking people to recall their memories of nights spent in bars presents a difficult task for a writer. The more one tends to enjoy an evening in such a place, the worse one's memory of it might be the next day—much less years later. So, I'm indebted to the number of people I interviewed for this book who generously provided their crystal clear memories of not only the Penthouse nightclub, but also deeper reflections on how much the city has changed over the decades.

In many ways, the seeds of this book were sown thirty-five years earlier by the hand of Joe Philliponi himself. During the 1976 trial, he started collecting daily newspaper clippings from *Vancouver Sun* and *Vancouver Province* writers like Denny Boyd, Jack Wasserman, Larry Still, and Lorne Parton regarding the trial and archived them in a massive scrapbook to which he later added a collection of Penthouse and Eagle Time articles going back to the 1940s. I was grateful to be entrusted with this scrapbook while researching and writing; it proved a considerable resource of dates and details that charted the sometimes blurred history of the bar. When drafting the text presented some complex or difficult crossroads, an article in the scrapbook often helped me navigate the way, and I could almost hear Joe himself directing me forward: "Kid, kid, kid, here's another good story for ya ..."

I was fortunate enough to have recorded hours of interviews in person, and in several telephone calls, with Ross Filippone in 2007. My late father had been a contemporary of Ross's, and as a lawyer had done

Joe Phillipone's Penthouse scrapbook.

Photo: Rebecca Blissett, 2012.

some legal work for the Filippones in the 1960s. This connection, and other family acquaintances, put him at ease with me, so that he spoke candidly—perhaps for the very first time—about the business his family had built and the (literal!) trials they went through while running it. Ross's keen memory was of great benefit to the book.

It is not uncommon in my experience that retired Vancouver police constables often feel reluctant to share their memories of the job with outsiders for a myriad of reasons. Beyond what often might be a distrust of the media, or a consideration of privacy issues, there are those who retire and simply do not want to relive the stresses or frustrations that are inherent to the service we ask of them. But their work gives them a unique perspective on the city that other citizens are not privy to, so I'm pleased that retired constables George Barclay, Leslie Schulze (McKellar), Bill Harkema and, in particular, Grant MacDonald and Vern Campbell, felt confident and comfortable enough to share their thoughts and memories of work, which often brought them into contact with members of the 1970s-era underworld in Vancouver who frequented the Penthouse.

Many thanks to Al Abraham, Bruce Allen, John Atkin, Rebecca Blissett, Gyles Brandreth (for the good advice), Drew Burns, Bob Burrows, Jack Card, Russ Chamberlain Q.C., Peter Chapman, Kenny Colman, Kelowna RCMP Cst. Chris Clark, Penny Crowe (Marks), Ray Culos, Tracey Davis, JoAnne Filippone, Rose Filippone (Fabbiano), Judge Thomas

Gove, Cst. Chris Graham (Ret.), Heritage Vancouver, Cst. Toby Hinton, James Johnstone, the Vancouver Police Museum, Sandy King, David and Duane Keogh, Barry Link and all at the *Vancouver Courier*, Jean-Paul Lorieau at the National Parole Board of Canada in Vancouver, all at the Commodore Ballroom and Live Nation Concerts Canada, John Mackie at the *Vancouver Sun*, Jana McGuinness and the Information and Privacy Unit at the Vancouver Police Department, Sean Mawhinney, Tony Pisani, Colin Preston at the CBC Archives in Vancouver, Edna Randle, Gwyn Roberts, Red Robinson, Capt. Gabe Roder at Vancouver Fire and Rescue Services, the Vancouver Public Library Special Collections Historical Photographs Section, Tevie Smith, and Will Woods at Forbidden Vancouver. My thanks also to those who preferred to remain off-the-record, providing additional documents, confidential reports, stories, and information that aided or confirmed the research in this book.

My great thanks to Brian Lam, Robert Ballantyne, Cynara Geissler, Susan Safyan, and Gerilee McBride at Arsenal Pulp Press for their faith, patience, enthusiasm, and professionalism with which they've undertaken the enterprise.

And lastly, but perhaps most of all, my gratitude goes to Danny Filippone, whose tireless support of seeing a Penthouse nightclub book published over the last several years is largely the reason you're reading this now. Danny and Arsenal put considerable trust in me to undertake the project, and Danny and other members of the Filippone family graciously

Joe standing in front of the Penthouse, 1957.

put up with my many phone calls and emails filled with questions and follow-up questions about their remarkable family. I hope Filippones past, present, and future will be pleased with the result.

I also hope that those who pass by the Penthouse building today will take a second look and see more than just a building with the metropolis burgeoning around it, and that they will think of the amazing stories and remarkable people who have been and continue to be behind its front door.

—Aaron Chapman

Prologue

1. from http://www.facebook.
com/VancouverSun/
posts/316239038387388?comment_
id=4576668

I. *Bella Fortuna*

2. Sturino, Franc. "Italians: Migration."
Multicultural Canada. [n.d.] http://www.
multiculturalcanada.ca/Encyclopedia/A-Z/
i11/2.

3. James Johnstone, "House History Report
[for 1033 Seymour Street]," 2008. Johnstone
found that the house was built in 1896 by
a Scottish-born contractor by the name of
Thomas Miller Rae, who purchased the lot
from the Canadian Pacific Railway company
in 1888. Rae's Presbyterian family had
arrived in Canada in 1884, and he and his
wife Jane and five children, as well as the
occasional lodger, lived in the house until
the 1920s, shortly before the Filippones
bought it.

4. "Fast Growing Delivery Service and Cab
Business in Modern Building," *Vancouver
Sun*, February 14, 1942.

5. Smith joined the Vancouver Police
Department, becoming one of its most

ENDNOTES

Filippone family photo, 1967. Front row, left–right:
Joey Filippone, Jimmy Jr Filippone, Teddy Pawlick Jr,
Danny Filippone, Penny Filippone, Maria Filippone,
Janie Filippone, Rose Filippone, Maria Rosa Filippone,
JoAnne Filippone, Josephine Filippone, Florence Pawlick,
Ross Filippone, Mickey Filippone, Joe Philliponi, Jimmy
Filippone, Ted Pawlick.

famous constables; he enjoyed a nation-wide reputation after appearing in the National Film Board documentary *Whistling Smith (Marrin Canell* and Michael Scott, 1975).

6. Cheryl Rossi, "Friend and Foe," *Vancouver Courier*, March 2, 2012.

7. Denny Boyd, "Joe Survived His First Showdown with a Gun," *Vancouver Sun*, September 21, 1983.

II. What Does a Guy Have to Do to Get a Drink Around Here?

8. "Population," *Canada Year Book 1955*. Ottawa: Dominion Bureau of Statistics, Canada Year Book Section, Information Services Division, 1955 and "Focus on Geography Series, 2011 Census," *Statistics Canada Catalogue no. 98-310-XWE2011004.* Ottawa: Statistics Canada, 2011.

9. Thomas, Dylan, *The Love Letters of Dylan Thomas,* Napierville, Ill: Sourcebooks, 2001.

10. Daniel Francis, *Red Light Neon*, Vancouver: Subway Books, 2006.

11. The Granville Street nightclub in Vancouver called Joe's Apartment is a tip of the hat to Joe Philliponi's old after-hours club.

12. Bottle clubs sold soft drinks; their customers brought in their own (concealed) alcohol.

13. Hal Straight, "From the Sun Tower," *Vancouver Sun*, July 28, 1947.

III. On with the Show

14. "We always brought ..." Jes Odam, "Death of a Friend Shocks Entertainers," *Vancouver Sun*, September 20, 1983.

15. Greg Potter and Red Robinson, *Backstage Vancouver* (Madeira Park, BC: Harbour Publishing, 2004).

16. Paul King, "He Picked It Out Himself—A Wonderful Place to Die," *Vancouver Sun*, October 16, 1959.

17. John Mackie, "Set 'Em Up Ross," *Vancouver Sun*, March 10, 2001.

IV. Life Is a Cabaret

18. Denny Boyd, "Legend Larger than the Man," *Vancouver Sun*, September 20, 1983.

V. Dollars and Sex

19. Allan Fotheringham, *Vancouver Sun*, December 22, 1977, p. 21.

20. Becki Ross, *Burlesque West: Showgirls, Sex, and Sin in Postwar Vancouver* (Toronto: University of Toronto Press, 2009), 58.

VI. Set 'Em Up

21. The author acknowledges the title of John Mackie's article, "Set 'Em Up, Ross," from the *Vancouver Sun*, March 10, 2001.

22. Daniel Francis, *Red Light Neon*, 89.

23. In 1973, then-Inspector Winterton led a crackdown on Granville Street prostitution, as reported in the November 16 *Vancouver Sun*.

24. Leslie McKellar was then Leslie Schulze.

25. Unpublished VPD investigation paper dated July 18, 1975, from Sergeant Beattie to Inspector Lake.

26. The author has chosen not to publish the man's name to protect his privacy.

27. Phil Benson is not his real name. The author has chosen not to publish the man's

name to protect his privacy.

28. According to the *Vancouver Sun* Sports Section race results from the next day.

29. In 2012, Detective Barclay told the author that the witness had simply identified the wrong Filippone brother.

30. Beckie Ross, *Burlesque West*, 79.

31. New York city mafioso Joe Valachi testified in 1963 to the US Senate about mafia history and its rituals, helping officials to crack a number of previously unsolved murder cases.

32. Larry Still, "Judge in Penthouse Spotlight," *Vancouver Sun*, October 9, 1976.

33. Denny Boyd, [title unknown.] *Vancouver Sun*, September 14, 1978.

34. Information and Privacy Unit Reference #12-1058A, filed May 10, 2012.

VII. The Show Must Go On

35. At one point he was acquitted of attempting to bribe a liquor inspector after giving the inspector a bottle of liquor.

VIII. *Buona Notte*

36. Larry Still, "Philliponi Calm at Gunpoint, Accused Says," *Vancouver Sun*, June 7, 1984.

37. Larry Still, "Philliponi Pleaded For Life, Court Told," *Vancouver Sun*, June 6, 1984.

38. Per VPD Constable Jana McGuinness, May 1, 2012, email to author.

39. "Little Cash in Safe, Court Told," *Globe and Mail*, May 11, 1984.

40. Caryl McBride, "Joe Will Be Missed Because He Was Always So Helpful," *Province*, September 21, 1985.

41. Rick Ouston, "Death of a Friend Shocks Entertainers," *Vancouver Sun*, September 20, 1983.

42. Denny Boyd, "Legend Larger Than The Man," *Vancouver Sun* September 20, 1983.

43. "Philliponi's Favors," *Westender*, September 22, 1983.

44. Neal Hall, "1980s Killer Always Said He Was Wrongly Convicted," *Vancouver Sun*, December 10, 2010.

IX. Changing of the Guard

45. "When Marilyn Manson ..." The author was playing at the Penthouse that night in the band The Town Pants as part of a New Music West Festival showcase, and remembers this incident as well.

46. Jimmy's boxing legacy is today remembered by Griffins Boxing and Fitness in North Vancouver; they established the "Jimmy Filippone Belt" in his honour, annually presented at their competitions.

47. Within seconds, friends and associates in attendance filled Danny Filippone's phone with messages to inform him of Jones's remarks.

REFERENCES

Books and Articles

Ackery, Ivan. *Fifty Years on Theatre Row*. North Vancouver, BC: Hancock House Publishers Ltd., 1980.

Barrett, Tom. "Cabaret Boss Philipponi Felt Persecuted by Police." *Vancouver Province*, April 19, 1977.

Boyd, Denny. "Joe Draws His Last Crow— and It's a Full House." *Vancouver Sun*, September 23, 1983.

———. [untitled]. *Vancouver Sun*, September 14, 1978.

———"Legend Larger Than the Man." *Vancouver Sun*, September 20, 1983.

———"Joe Survived His First Showdown with a Gun." *Vancouver Sun*, September 21, 1983.

———"The Death of this Tough Guy is Curve Ball for the Celestial Jury." *Vancouver Sun*, August 11, 1983.

Brooks, Jack. "800 Mourners Gather to Remember Slain Joe." *Vancouver Sun*, September 22, 1983.

Canada. Dominion Bureau of Statistics. Canada Year Book Section. Information Services Division. "Population." *Canada Year Book 1955*. Ottawa: Canada Year Book, 1955.

1945–46 Diamond Cabs Bowling Champions

Canada. Statistics Canada. "Focus on Geography Series, 2011 Census." *Statistics Canada Catalogue No. 98-310-XWE2011004.* Ottawa: Statistics Canada, 2011.

Chapman, Aaron. "Strip off the Old Block." *Vancouver Courier*, February 6, 2008.

Conner, Shawn. "Big Italy." *Westender*, June 21, 2012.

Davis, Chuck, ed. *The Greater Vancouver Book: An Urban Encyclopedia.* Surrey, BC: Linkman Press, 1997.

Didon, Pino. "Philliponi Disappoves of Nudity." *L'Eco Italia*, January 20, 1978.

Dylan, Thomas. *The Love Letters of Dylan Thomas.* Napierville, Ill: Sourcebooks, 2001.

Fairley, Jim. "Penthouse Operators Guilty in Cabaret Vice Conspiracy." *Vancouver Province*, April 23, 1977.
———. "FBI Agent Had Heard of Penthouse." *Vancouver Province*, April 29, 1977.

"Fast Growing Delivery Service and Cab Business in Modern Building." *Vancouver Sun*, February 14, 1942.

Faustman, John. "Joe Philliponi's World." *Vancouver Courier*, August 12, 1979.

Fotheringham, Allan. [untitled.] *Vancouver Sun*, December 22, 1977.

Francis, Daniel. *Red Light Neon: A History of Vancouver's Sex Trade.* Vancouver: Subway Books, 2006.

Hall, Neal. "1980s Killer Always Said He Was Wrongly Convicted." *Vancouver Sun*, December 10, 2010.

Hill, Mary Frances. "Penthouse Bumps, Grinds in New Era." *Westender*, January 17, 2002.

Jiwa, Salim, and Suzanne Fournier. "He Beat All the Raps." *Vancouver Province*, September 20, 1983.
———. "Joe's Mom Will Be Absent." *Vancouver Province*, September 22, 1983.

Johnstone, James. "History of the House at 1033 Seymour." *Home History Research.* 2008.

King, Paul. "He Picked It Out Himself—A Wonderful Place to Die." *Vancouver Sun*, October 16, 1959.

"Little Cash in Safe, Court Told." *Globe and Mail*, May 11, 1984.

Loranger, Clancy. "It Says Here." *Vancouver Province*, February 2, 1943.

Lytle, Andy. "Now He's Uncle Joe to Hundreds." *Vancouver Sun*, December 8, 1949.

Mackie, John. "Set 'Em Up, Ross." *Vancouver Sun*, March 10, 2001.
———. "Surviving on the Strip: Penthouse Reaches 60." *Vancouver Sun*, September 29, 2007.

McBride, Caryl. "Joe Will Be Missed Because He Was Always So Helpful." *Vancouver Province*, September 21, 1983.

McGillivray, Alex. [title unknown.] Leisure Section. *Vancouver Sun*, December 20, 1968.

McRae, Scott. "Tints and Tones of The Penthouse Trial." *Vancouver Sun*, October 22, 1976.

Moore, Vincent. *Angelo Branca, Gladiator of the Courts*. Vancouver: Douglas & McIntyre, 1981.

Odam, Jes. "Death of a Friend Shocks Entertainers." *Vancouver Sun*, September 20, 1983.

Ouston, Rick. "The Show Goes On." *Vancouver Sun*, September 20, 1983.
———. "IOUs Said Missing from Victim's Safe." *Vancouver Sun*, September 21, 1983.
———. "Grandmothers, Strippers Mingle as Penthouse Hosts Wake for Joe." *Vancouver Sun*, September 23, 1983.

"Police Raids Gather in 9 Bottles." *Vancouver Province*, December 4, 1950.

Parton, Lorne. "Old Days and Nights Were Long Ago." *Vancouver Province*, September 20, 1983.

"'Penthouse' Visited by Police Dry Squad—Officers Swoop Down on Second Day of Operation of New Cabaret." *Vancouver Sun*, December 4, 1950.

"Philliponi's Favors." *Westender*, September 22, 1983.

"Philliponi Will Face New Charges—Soft Drink Sale Without License; Drinking in Public." *Vancouver Sun*, July 23, 1949.

Potter, Greg, and Red Robinson. *Backstage Vancouver: A Century of Entertainment Legends*. Madeira Park, BC: Harbour Publishing, 2004.

Poulsen, Chuck. "Penthouse Hangout for Local Mafia." *Vancouver Province*. September 11, 1976.

Ross, Becki L. *Burlesque West: Showgirls, Sex and Sin in Postwar Vancouver*. Toronto: University of Toronto Press, 2009.

Rossi, Cheryl. "Friend and Foe." *Vancouver Courier*, March 2, 2012.

Salmi, Brian: "Hooker History: 125 Years of Illegal Sex and the City." *Georgia Straight*, November 2–9, 2000.

Smith, Dave. "Freed Philliponi Suspect: A Contract Out On Me." *Vancouver Sun*, September 21, 1983.

Still, Larry. "Penthouse Initiation Began on First Night, Prostitute Testifies." *Vancouver Sun*, September 2, 1976.
———. "Penthouse Trail Told Local Mafia Tried Takeover." *Vancouver Sun*, September 11, 1976.
———. "Kind of a Union Shop for Hookers." *Vancouver Sun*, September 18, 1976.
———. "Tape Recording Made in Penthouse Covers Politics, Sex." *Vancouver Sun*, September 21, 1976.
———. "Prostitute Witness Tells Penthouse Trial, 'I Cherish My Life.'" *Vancouver Sun*, September 22, 1976.
———. "Prostitute was Police Woman." *Vancouver Sun*, September 23, 1976.
———. "Penthouse Prostitute Accused of 'Concocting' Evidence." *Vancouver Sun*, September 28, 1976.
———. "Penthouse Probe Officer Led Champagne Existence." *Vancouver Sun*, September 30, 1976.
———. "Judge in Penthouse Spotlight." *Vancouver Sun*, October 9, 1976.
———. "Penthouse Defence Lawyer to Call Witnesses Concerning Perjury Allegation." *Vancouver Sun*, October 13, 1976.
———. "Names Drop Like Rain in Filippone Testimony." *Vancouver Sun*, December 18, 1976.
———. "Crown Calls the Penthouse 'A Scandal in This Community.'" *Vancouver Sun*, February 25, 1977.
———. "Cabaret 5 Cleared." *Vancouver Sun*, December 20, 1977.
———. "Penthouse Drama $2 Million Morality Play." *Vancouver Sun*, December 21, 1977.
———. "Penthouse Cabaret Will Reopen." *Vancouver Sun*, September 14, 1978.

———. "Voice on Tape Details Death of Philliponi." *Vancouver Sun*, June 1, 1984.

———. "Philliponi Pleaded for Life, Court Told." *Vancouver Sun*, June 6, 1984.

———. "Philliponi Calm at Gunpoint Accused Says." *Vancouver Sun*, June 7, 1984.

———. "At Least 25 Years Behind Bars Facing Two Killers of Philliponi." June 14, 1984.

Straight, Hal. "From the Sun Tower." *Vancouver Sun*, July 28, 1947.

Sturino, Franc. "Italians: Migration." *Multicultural Canada*. [n.d.] http://www.multiculturalcanada.ca/Encyclopedia/A-Z/i11/2.

Wasserman, Jack. "Quickniks." *Vancouver Sun*, December 22, 1975.

———. "Notes to Me." *Vancouver Sun*, September 15, 1976.

Wiseman, Les. "Not Your Average Joe." *Vancouver* (April 1982): 60–64, 68, 84.

———. "Young, Sexy and Well-Heeled." *Vancouver* (March 1982): 29–31, 33–35, 145.

Yeager, Sherryl: "The Penthouse that Joe Built." *Vancouver Courier*, January 21, 1996.

Unpublished Documents

National Parole Board Pre-Release Decision Sheet for Scott Ogilvie Forsyth. Panel Review. NPD 82 (99–05), April 30, 2004.

Vancouver Police Department: Investigation Division, Penthouse Cabaret, 1019 Seymour Street. To: Inspector J.S.V. Lake, i/c Vice Section, from Sergeant M. Beattie. July 18, 1975.

Her Majesty The Queen against Celebrity Enterprises Ltd., Joseph Philliponi, Ross Filippone, Domenick Filippone, Jan Sedlak, Minerva Kelly, Rose Filippone. County Court Case No. 760706.

Freedom of Information Request to VPD. Information & Privacy Unit Reference 12–1058A, with cover letter dated July 25, 2012 to author from Civilian Analyst VA9426.

Television

Joe Philliponi and Jack Wasserman, *Hourglass*, CBC Television, 53:03. Broadcast June 27, 1977.

Interviews

Al Abraham, interviewed in Vancouver, May 14, 2012.

Bruce Allen, telephone interview, May 1, 2012.

Cst. George Barclay, Ret., telephone interview, July 12, 2012.

Bob Burrows, interviewed in Vancouver, March 9, 2012.

Robert Campell, PhD, interviewed in Vancouver, May 11, 2012.

Cst. Vern Campbell, Ret., interviewed in Vancouver, March 23, 2012.

Russ Chamberlain, interviewed in Richmond, BC, May 26, 2012.

RCMP Kelowna Cst. Chris Clark, telephone interview, July 12, 2012.

Rose Fabbiano, telephone interview, April 25, 2012.

Danny Filippone, interviewed in Vancouver, January 26, 2007.

Danny Filippone, interviewed in Vancouver, July 14, 2012.

JoAnne Filippone, telephone interview, April 18, 2012.

Ross Filippone, interviewed in Vancouver, February 6, 2007.

Ross Filippone, telephone interview, March, 2007.

Cst. Bill Harkema, Ret., interviewed in Vancouver, April 30, 2012.

Sandy King, interviewed in Vancouver, May 17, 2012.

Penny Marks, interviewed in Vancouver, June 13, 2012.

Mike McCardell, interviewed in Vancouver, April 2, 2012.

Cst. Grant MacDonald, Ret., interviewed in Vancouver, March 28, 2012.

Cst. Jana McGuinness, email interview, May 1, 2012.

Tony Pisani, interviewed in Vancouver, March 11, 2012.

Edna Randle, interviewed in Vancouver, May 17, 2012

Leslie McKellar, telephone interview, March, 2007.

Tevie Smith, interviewed in Vancouver, May 21, 2012.

Note: Page numbers in **bold** denote photos.

INDEX

Ross with actor Vincent Pastore.

AARON CHAPMAN

Aaron Chapman is a writer, historian, and musician with a special interest in Vancouver's entertainment history. Born and raised in Vancouver, he has been a contributor to the *Vancouver Courier*, the *Georgia Straight*, and CBC Radio. A graduate of the University of British Columbia, he is also a member of Heritage Vancouver and the Point Roberts Historical Society. *aaronchapman.net*

Photo: Rebecca Blissett.